What Dr Gary Wood's students say .

Gary is an exceptionally gifted teacher who has the ability to meet people where they are. He is ethical, kind, compassionate, insightful, and witty. I learnt a great deal (content and process) from him.

Carol Hughes, therapeutic counsellor

Without doubt, the most knowledgeable and engaging lecturer I have ever been taught by. Great energy, great enthusiasm and made learning real fun for the group.

Andrea Burns, senior HR practitioner

Gary's teaching style made me feel relaxed from day one and he is an extremely engaging teacher. I also felt that the feedback given was invaluable and enabled me to progress from feeling extremely nervous handing in my first assignment to handing in work that produced first class grades.

Helen Wallis, yoga teacher

Gary's unique insight into psychological theory, along with his lively and entertaining delivery of teaching materials, led me to develop a keen interest in psychological research. I eventually went on to achieve a PhD in Psychology, something I do not think I would have done without that initial spark of interest that Gary instilled in me.

Dr Natalie Kelly, lecturer in Psychology

Gary is the one lecturer that I simply never forget. He somehow managed to turn dry theory into whole class funtime. So, when I'm scanning my brain to remember . . . psychological theories: it's all there, because the whole class sort of acted it out and made it real.

Holly Nolan, arts in health facilitator

During my undergraduate studies, Dr Gary Wood equipped me with skills in evaluating evidence, synthesising information, and developing clear written arguments, which I continued to use right up to PhD level. He led dynamic discussions which stretched my cohort to reach their potential. I count him among the best teachers I've had at any stage of my education.

Dr Kate Mascarenhas, researcher and novelist

Gary is a knowledgeable and engaging tutor. His books and coaching skills have helped me develop both personally and professionally.

Lydia Matheson, head librarian

Gary has excellent presentation skills which engage students of different ages, abilities and backgrounds. He communicates both enthusiasm for and great insight into his subject. From him I learnt not only about academic evidence-based psychology, but also additional practical research skills.

Adrian Rhodes, management consultant

Dr Gary Wood's teaching methods were captivating, inspiring and entertaining. My journey with education has continued to this day. I found Gary's approach informative and he created a fantastic atmosphere in class.

Liz Pugh, business management student

Dr Wood is one of those rare personalities who are able to both enlighten and inspire. I can, without any exaggeration, say that it is because of Dr Wood that I began taking a deeper interest in psychology as a subject and that his unique approach to teaching and demonstrating has helped me throughout my life as a practitioner, teacher, and trainer.

Hamid Shahid Khan, corporate trainer and author

What Dr Gary Wood's colleagues say . . .

Having worked with Gary over many years in a range of teaching environments from adults working professionally in the sexual health field, to school children, to foster carers. His skill in accommodating a range of learning styles on one-to-one basis small and large groups is outstanding. And, using a range of professional skills and humour to overcome challenging circumstances.

Jan Deeming, sexual health training and community outreach professional

Gary Wood is an exciting and interesting communicator, who gets across a message in a memorable way. He collaborated on the design and delivery . . . of a really innovative programme that fired up the enthusiasm of the participants – and this was largely due to Gary's teaching style and excellent abilities to communicate.

Dr Anita Pickerden, interview coach and author

Gary worked with me on a Management Development Programme . . . He created a vibrant and engaging experiential approach to team building. I could always rely on Gary's knowledge, professionalism, energy, and sense of humour to provide a great learning experience for our students.

Alan Clark, management coach, author and trainer

Gary Wood has built a career in supporting other people in practical and compassionate ways. As a tutor his style of teaching is popular with students of all abilities and ages because it starts from a position of working out what their needs are and building their confidence from their starting point . . . Gary makes a point of ensuring both the big and small stuff gets attention, so students don't overlook core skills but also don't get caught up worrying about things they already have the ability to fix. He ensures people have the resources, networks and insights to move at their own pace and to stretch themselves so they find they can achieve way more than they imagined.

Dr Petra Boynton, social psychologist, agony aunt and author

LETTERS TO
A NEW STUDENT

Letters to a New Student is a study skills book with a twist. You decide how to read it.

Based on a series of short, informal, problem-page style letters that you can read in any order, the book uses principles of human psychology, teaching, and coaching practice to offer a refreshing approach to study skills and learning techniques. The letters form a brief 'survive and thrive' study guide to work smarter not harder and offer advice on topics such as motivation, stress, revision, and assignments. It's a tried-and-tested, blueprint to make information stick with less effort.

The book takes a holistic approach to learning. It covers health and wellbeing, the 'nuts-and-bolts' shortcuts, the obstacles, and the pitfalls. It also includes short learning principles and cross-references to other entries, with practical tips in response to the frequently asked questions by students during their studies.

Letters to a New Student is for any student under pressure, parents and family who want to offer support, or anyone with interest in lifelong learning. It's written by a psychologist, teacher, academic coach, and advice columnist, with over 20 years professional experience.

Dr Gary W. Wood is a Chartered Psychologist, solution-focused life coach and broadcaster. He is Fellow of the Higher Education Academy and has taught psychology, research methods, and learning skills in several UK universities. Gary appears in the media offering expert analysis and coaching tips and as an agony uncle (advice columnist). To find out more visit: www.drgarywood.co.uk

LETTERS TO A NEW STUDENT

Tips to Study Smarter
from a Psychologist

Dr Gary W. Wood

Routledge
Taylor & Francis Group

LONDON AND NEW YORK

First published 2019
by Routledge
2 Park Square, Milton Park, Abingdon, Oxon OX14 4RN

and by Routledge
711 Third Avenue, New York, NY 10017

Routledge is an imprint of the Taylor & Francis Group, an informa business

British Library Cataloguing-in-Publication Data
A catalogue record for this book is available from the British Library

Library of Congress Cataloging-in-Publication Data
A catalog record for this book has been requested

ISBN: 978-1-138-36253-6
ISBN: 978-1-138-36254-3
ISBN: 978-0-429-43202-6

Typeset in Bembo
by Florence Production Ltd, Stoodleigh, Devon, EX16 9PN

Printed and bound in Great Britain by
TJ International Ltd, Padstow, Cornwall

CONTENTS

ACKNOWLEDGMENTS

Thank you to everyone who supported the writing process, especially Eleanor Reedy at Routledge (Taylor and Francis) for championing the book, and for her constructive suggestions about the text and the exchanges we had along the way. Thanks also to Alex Howard, Kris Siosyte and the Routledge team, Ting Baker for copy editing, Meridith L. Murray for the index and Iain Campbell for his feedback in shaping the book's early development.

I am also indebted to all my students over the years for their questions, feedback and endorsements. Thanks to the Society of Authors for contractual advice and invaluable support during my writing career.

Immeasurable thanks, as always, to Dr Takeshi Fujisawa for his practical and technical support, encouragement, patience, and cake.

This book is dedicated to my grandparents. From my granddad Clifford Bertram Butcher, I inherited my love of books and from my 'Nan', Nelly Florence Butcher, I enjoyed hours of indulgence as a child where I was the teacher and she was my pupil. This book is another opportunity for me to 'pay it forward'.

It is also dedicated to Janet Claire Deeming (1955–2018), an inspirational colleague, friend, and 'human library'. She was one of a kind and sorely missed. Jan spent her life helping other people. A total professional, her almost forensic preparation contrasted with her open, inclusive, and relaxed style of training delivery. I learned a great deal from her and we shared a lot of laughs on numerous excursions with her trusty chauffeur, Parker.

(The three underrated RCA albums by the late, great David Cassidy (1950–2017) were the playlist for writing this book.)

PREFACE

Inspiration comes from unlikely sources. It's almost as if the brain has a mind of its own – always working in the background.

The idea for a learning and study skills book based on a series of letters came from reading Rainer Maria Rilke's *Letters to a Young Poet,* and *The Screwtape Letters* by C. S. Lewis. There's also a bit of 'dice-living', from Luke Rhinehart's *The Dice Man* thrown in to create a similar experience as the old *Dungeons and Dragons* books.

Inspiration comes not only from what we read but also from the people we meet and the things we do in life. Learning is about how we transform our knowledge and experience.

I wanted to create a book that I'd like to read and one that gives a sense of being in one of my classes or workshops.

And, you don't have to be a student to get something from this book. Many of its principles also apply to life, generally.

It's not taken nearly as long to write it as it has to live it. May it give you a shortcut to success.

Best wishes and bright moments,

Buying books would be a good thing if one could also buy the time to read them in: but as a rule, the purchase of books is mistaken for the appropriation of their contents.

Arthur Schopenhauer (1788–1860),
philosopher

AN INTRO
OF SORTS ...

Letters to a New Student is a study skills book with a difference: you choose how to read it.

It's also brief.

As a student faced with a daunting reading list, the last thing you need is yet another book 'thick enough to stun an ox'. Or, if you need to offer to support to a student, you'll also want to cut to the chase' for helpful tips.

Reading a study skills book can save a lot of trial and error. And yet, many students resist the idea. It can be hard to give up on our own way of doing things. It's often 'better the devil you know'! And, it's also tough to accept that things could have been easier.

The book is written in plain English and in short, bite-sized pieces – Q & A letters. It offers the main principles of learning I wish I'd been told when I started out. The book aims to get you to work smarter rather than harder; to work with basic human psychology rather than fight it.

Read it from cover-to-cover. Read the short sections in *any* order to create your meaningful path. Dip in and out for 'learning hacks' to top-up your existing approach. Use it as a troubleshooting guide. Chart a random course by rolling dice! Mix and match. The choice is yours. No matter the order you read it, you get the same blueprint for learning how to learn.

If you're in a hurry, just read the 'nutshell' section and skip the rest of the intro.

The book 'in a nutshell'

- We process information better when we know what to expect. So, before you carry on, flick through to get an idea of the layout the book, then come back here.

- After this introduction, the book has 11 themed chapters: each covers an aspect of learning and studying. It takes about ten minutes to read each one.

- A chapter begins with a one-line summary and a quotation to set the scene.

- Chapters contain a series of letters based on frequently asked questions (FAQs).

- These letters are written in an informal, problem-page format – like a magazine advice column. Each one takes just two to three minutes to read.

- For each letter, there's a question from 'a student' and a response from me.

- The questions are composites of the things students have asked me over the years.

- After each Q & A, there's a key summary learning point. There are also six signposts to other letters that connect and overlap.

- To help you find you way around the book there's a contents page, at the start, with brief descriptions of the chapters. At the back, there's a standard index.

- For extra help, at the end, there's a quick-fire summary of the main learning principles. There's also an open-book exam to test what you've learned or guide your reading.

- The main chapters are numbered two to 12, so you can roll a pair of dice to decide where to start or go next. There are six signposts after each letter, if you can't choose, just use a single dice to do it for you.

- At the end of each chapter there's a checklist to help you keep track of what you've read.

Main aims

The book aims to encourage a deeper approach to learning where you take an active interest to transform the knowledge in some way to understand things for yourself, instead of just trying to 'playback' stuff like a recording device. It also aims to help you to organize and manage time more effectively, and how to play by the rules.

Main themes

To help you to meet these aims

A. **Foundation** – *to get fit and ready to learn* see Chapters 2 (Attitudes), 3 (Stress) and 4 (Wellbeing).

B. **Managing obstacles** – *to have a less bumpy ride* see Chapters 5 (Motivation), 8 (Emotions) and 12 (Support).

C. **Practical psychology** – *for the nitty-gritty, nuts and bolts* see Chapters 6 (Cognition), 7 (Context), 9 (Techniques), 10 (Assignments) and 11 (Revision).

Decisions, decisions

The story of how the book came about, follows.

Read on, skip it and jump to Chapter 2 (Attitudes). Roll a pair of dice. Your choice.

The vaguely, inspiring, and informative but entirely optional and 'skippable' whimsical back-story

In order to change a colour, it is enough to change the colour of its background.

Michel Eugene Chevreul (1786–1889),
chemist and writer

The book's approach came about from my personal and professional journey, first as a student, then as a teacher. It started with my return to education as a mature student – a night class in psychology. I'd always battled with the 'no-pain-no-gain' way of learning. It was often very painful; the gains were hit-and-miss and rarely worth all the effort. But, it didn't occur to me there could be any other way. But this time I had the idea that psychology must have tips on studying itself. It was pre-Internet, and at that time, there were no study skills books on the market. Instead, I made do with a psychology textbook. I found a few ideas on attitudes, attention span, the context of learning, and how to take a more holistic approach to studying. This modest find inspired me to look for more hints and to apply what I found. This time around, I was more focused, more confident, wasted less time and did much, much better in the exam.

One minor event was a major turning point for me. One evening I couldn't attend the class, and there was a power cut. Nothing to do with me! The lecturer told me the following week that while they all sat in the dark, a fellow student said, 'If Gary were here, he'd know what to do'. I probably wouldn't have, but it was lovely that someone thought so. Classmates had also begun to ask me questions, mostly about statistics. I was happy to help. Insights deepen when we explain things to others. That part-time course led to another, then to a degree in psychology, to teaching training, to a PhD, and a teaching job.

My approach to study skills grew as I worked with a broader range of students. My first trial by fire was teaching research methods to psychology students. Mostly, they hate statistics. The subject sparks strong negative emotions such as fear and frustration, and because we strive to avoid such feelings, they act as barriers to learning. The students' horror was made worse as they had to learn to use a software package. I spent hours honing the 'perfect' hand-out. It was a step-by-step, booklet that aimed to allay fears, build confidence, and offer clear guidance for anything the students would need. I presumed they would read it. Halfway through the term, a student asked a question. I answered it and pointed to the relevant bit in the handout. She looked up, threw her head back, laughed, and said, 'No one reads handouts, they're just there to look pretty in your folder!' That's when I grasped that in times of stress we need the quickest fix. On the other hand, if we want to absorb information better, we need to relax. That lesson came next.

Later, I began teaching a night class in psychology for mature-aged students. When the time came to teach research methods, I broke the number one rule. For the first class, I prepared nothing. I'd also started work as a magazine advice columnist (agony uncle) and thought I'd try a less formal style in class. There was no script, just me, a few marker pens and a blank whiteboard. Instead of the usual 'trip to the morgue', students laughed about stats! Also, I got a boost in confidence as I put myself on the spot. I realized how well I knew the stuff. It also reinforced how important our attitudes are for learning. From then on, every new intake of students had the relaxed chat to kick-off the research methods course.

Without a doubt, the Internet has changed how we get information – answers in a split-second. Or sometimes we might amble along, clicking links until we find ourselves watching videos of cute cats or blackhead popping, with no idea how we got there. This book mimics this 'stream of consciousness' style. But, unlike the limitless ocean of the Internet, the covers of the book are the walls of the aquarium.

Your cover-to-cover path continues with the topic of attitudes (Chapter 2, pp. 7–14) and how they shape your view of the world and your approach to learning.

(And just in case you read this last, I hope you enjoyed the book, and best wishes in your academic career . . . and life in general.)

ATTITUDES

How attitudes shape
how we learn

It is our attitude at the beginning of a difficult task which, more than anything else, will affect its successful outcome.
William James (1842–1910),
philosopher and psychologist

A: How do I break the ice and make a good first impression?

Q *The first day of my new course is looming. I'm dreading it. I'm usually confident but feel well out of my comfort zone – like a very small fish in a very big pond. I won't know anyone, and I don't want to make a bad impression. Any advice so I don't come across as an idiot?*

A When faced with new situations it's useful to take a deep breath and take stock of the times you feel more confident. What do you do differently at these times? Now think about the times when you felt a little less sure of yourself but got through them anyway. Focus on what's worked before and see how you could use it again.

On the first day, everyone will be, pretty much, in the same boat. However, two things can give you an edge and create a good impression, before you say a word. First, get a good night's sleep. Yawns and puffy, half-closed eyes are not great social invitations. Second, smile! The mean, moody and sultry look might work for celebrities, but it won't help you to make friends. If you can't manage a relaxed smile, don't go for the 'wait until they get a load of me' full-on rictus grin. Just turn-up the corners of your mouth and raise your eyebrows. People do it all the time. A smile makes you feel better, and it helps to put others at ease. It signals a lack of threat and can make you look more approachable, likeable, and more attractive.

In new or awkward situations, most people wait for someone else to make the first move. Be that person! Don't agonize over what to say. It doesn't have to be clever, witty, or wise. People won't remember what you said, just that you made an effort to break the ice. A simple hello is enough. Then just say who you are and ask who they are. That's it. It's the central principle of my confidence-building approach that we boost our own confidence as we focus on building it in others. So, follow-up with questions such as 'What are you looking forward to most about being here?' Or 'How do you like to spend your time?' Use questions that put people at ease and evoke positive emotions for them. Their good feelings become part of your first impression. Research shows that when you come across as a warm person, it creates a halo effect. As a result, other positive traits are ascribed to you too, such as intelligence. It's the same for all new social situations. That's got to raise a smile, surely?

Learning principle

 Take stock of past successes to pinpoint useful skills for new situations, don't overthink, be brave, smile and be the one who breaks the ice.[1]

Connections and overlaps

 Carry on reading in order, choose one of the following or roll a dice:

1. Stress (Chapter 3, pp. 15–21)
2. Motivation (Chapter 5, pp. 31–40)
3. Context (Chapter 7, pp. 51–57)
4. Cognition (Chapter 6, pp. 41–49)
5. Support (Chapter 12, pp. 95–102)
6. Assignments (Chapter 10, pp. 77–86)

B: Missing out on the good life?

Q *I'm stuck indoors churning out coursework like a sausage machine, slogging away and cramming for exams, and my friends have jobs. They now earn good money and live the high life while I live a life of abject poverty and misery and always turn down invitations. I know you are going to say it will all be worth it in the end. But what about now?*

A In coaching, I use the phrase 'The viewing influences the doing, and vice versa'. The sausage machine mindset colours your view of learning. There is not a positive way to think of a sausage machine, unless you really, really like sausage! Attitude means 'fit and ready for action'. Attitudes are like starting blocks for a runner – the 'on your marks, get set' before they go. At the most basic level, they frame our experiences as likes and dislikes. So, if you see learning as 'missing out' it only creates resentment. It's not a wonderful way to start, and it's not likely to propel you forward. It's good that you recognize 'it will be all worth it in the end'. Build on that. Review, regularly, how it will be all worth it.

You currently see learning in terms of loss, not as an opportunity, or a luxury. How might things change if you adopted those attitudes? Instead, research tells us that the wording of questions affects what we focus on and how we recall information. With coaching clients, I begin sessions with the question 'What's been better?' to make sure we capture the good stuff then build on it. Emotions colour our experiences, and things sink in better if we start with a positive mindset. So, rather than resentment, create a better metaphor such as a machine producing luxury goods. Focus on the privilege it is to study rather than restriction and loss. This becomes easier if you can give studying a personal relevance. What can you do to take control, make it more meaningful and enjoyable to you?

If you're doing it right, studying doesn't mean giving up all else. It just means you get the balance right, so you work when you're supposed to but still make time for play. If money is an issue, talk to your friends and plan things that won't cost too much. Often, it's not what you do; it's who you do it with. So, be creative, look for free events, make the most of student discounts, voucher deals and support local talent.

Learning principle

 Your attitudes define your experience of the world, and of learning for better or worse.[2]

Connections and overlaps

 Carry on reading in order, choose one of the following or roll a dice:

1. Emotions (Chapter 8, pp. 59–66)
2. Motivation (Chapter 5, pp. 31–40)
3. Context (Chapter 7, pp. 51–57)
4. Stress (Chapter 3, pp. 15–21)
5. Cognition (Chapter 6, pp. 41–49)
6. Support (Chapter 12, pp. 95–102)

C: Getting on top of things before they get on top of you

Q *I hate most of the subjects I'm studying. Most of the time I feel swamped and out of control. I'm putting on a brave face and keep myself to myself as I don't want people to think I'm thick or a failure. I think I hide it well and really envy those who seem to find it easy. Every few weeks I feel like I want to give up on it but somehow manage to muddle through by clinging on to the few subjects I like. What can I do to get on top of things?*

A Everyone studying, at some point, will feel like giving up. It's part of the process. It's a sign that you've pushed beyond the limits of what you know. Thinking about giving up is a defence mechanism, a reminder that you do have a choice. You can come up with a brand-new life plan, or you can take a deep breath, dig in and make this one work. If you stay on this path, start with a review of your reasons for studying. Any journey needs a destination in mind. Review the pay-offs often. Make a poster and display it as a constant reminder of your future, desired outcome.

Your attitudes can create a buffer against stress. Researchers studied people in risky and stressful jobs, such as firefighters, to see how they coped. They found three core attitudes helped – the three Cs. These are *control, commitment* and *challenge*. Together they make *psychological hardiness*, a kind of resilience that you can apply to studying.

The opposite of control is powerlessness. When faced with tough goals, if you focus on your lack of power, you'll find a lot of reasons to support that view. Instead, take stock and list all under your control. Start with the small stuff, however obvious it seems. Then reflect on what tiny steps will help you to gain control.

Commitment is about making connections, and the opposite is 'cutting yourself off', or as you put it 'keeping to yourself'. Instead, commit to connect with other people and have curiosity about the world. Passive learners stay indoors and wait for the rain to stop. Active learners grab an umbrella and get out there! An easy way to connect is to ask questions – these can help to guide your reading or to get information from tutors and peers. A fellow student might explain things in a way that makes more sense to you. Never be afraid to let others 'show-off'. It deepens their understanding as they explain it. You're really doing them a favour!

The opposite of challenge is security, that is, playing it safe in your comfort zone. Studying your pet topics has a built-in reward. It's nice to spend time doing something you like. By contrast, you spend less time on the tough stuff. Your challenge for less familiar topics is to find 'your way in'. Go back to basics and review what you do understand. Look for anything, however small that sparks your curiosity. Set bite-sized goals to learn basic terms, like learning a second language. Look for connections between the abstract information and how it relates to the concrete, real-world. Again, actively engage other people to check your understanding. Given a chance, and adopting the three Cs, could mean that your feared topics become your favourites. Studying is not that different from making friends.

Learning principle

 Adopting the attitudes of commitment, control and challenge can help to create a buffer against stress in times of change and uncertainty.[3]

Connections and overlaps

 Carry on reading in order, choose one of the following or roll a dice:

1. Emotions (Chapter 8, pp. 59–66)
2. Stress (Chapter 3, pp. 15–21)
3. Support (Chapter 12, pp. 95–102)
4. Motivation (Chapter 5, pp. 31–40)
5. Wellbeing (Chapter 4, pp. 23–30)
6. Assignments (Chapter 10, pp. 77–86)
7. Revision (Chapter 11, pp. 87–94)

D: Give me a quick-fix confidence boost

Q *I'm usually calm until a few minutes before an event. I'm then plagued by self-doubts and go to pieces. Any quick fix tips to counter this?*

A Our confidence ebbs and flows all the time depending on situations and moods. By pinpointing times your confidence is higher, you can identify what you do differently. You can then extend that to low confidence situations. Low confidence and 'having a downer' on yourself is a form of self-prejudice. You pre-judge before you've given yourself a chance. Here's a quick-fix to counter those negative attitudes and self-doubts. Use it before exams, interviews, presentations or even first dates.

Take a deep breath, set a timer for 60 seconds and then say out loud all your skills, strengths, successes, and positive qualities. If you're feeling brave, do it in the mirror. Try to say as many different things, but it doesn't matter if you repeat things. The main thing is you do it for a minute non-stop. When the time's up, smile! You're now ready to go.

Learning principle

 In times of lower confidence, take stock of your strengths, skills, and successes.[4]

Connections and overlaps

 Carry on reading in order, choose one of the following or roll a dice:

1. Emotions (Chapter 8, pp. 59–66)
2. Stress (Chapter 3, pp. 15–21)
3. Support (Chapter 12, pp. 95–102)
4. Motivation (Chapter 5, pp. 31–40)
5. Wellbeing (Chapter 4, pp. 23–30)
6. Revision (Chapter 11, pp. 87–94)

Summary and what's next

Attitudes affect how you absorb and process information and create a buffer against change and uncertainty. Positive mental attitudes can make it easier to learn and increase the chance that you'll succeed.

In the next section, we look at stress, how it affects how you process information, and why a little stress can be a good thing.

Checklist

Keep a track of which letters you've read.

A   Read it   ☐
B   Read it   ☐
C   Read it   ☐
D   Read it   ☐

STRESS

How stress affects learning, how to relax, and why a little stress is a good thing

If water derives lucidity from stillness, how much more the faculties of the mind.

Zhuang Zhou (also known as Chuang Tzu, 369 BCE–286 BCE), philosopher

[*Please note*: This material is for general information only and does not replace dedicated expert advice for your emotional and mental health needs. If in doubt, seek professional support.]

A: How can I stay calmer?

Q *Help! My head is spinning. I'm in a constant state of panic. I've tried lots of things to become calmer, but there's no way I can sit still for 20 minutes trying to clear my mind. Thoughts pop into my head, and I end up feeling worse.*

Am I just not the kind of person this works for? What else can I do?

A We think of top athletes as always 'on the go'. Yet, the fastest people on earth also learn how to slow down first. They use relaxation techniques to control their physiology. Pretty much the same applies when our minds begin to race. The opposite of stress is relaxation. They can't both occur at the same time. So, you won't relax if you stress about 'getting it right'. There are no prizes for perfection in meditation. There is no one-size-fits-all. You just need to approach it with an attitude of openness, work with the basic principles and find what works for you.

Let's strip it down to the basics. Think of how, automatically, you take a deep breath to prepare for a challenge. You might also close your eyes to 'collect your thoughts'. Build on these 'micro-meditations'. If 20 minutes doesn't suit your routine, at first, start small. Little and often will help create a habit. To gauge how well it works for you, try this out for a week or two. In confidence-building workshops, I begin with a two-minute stress-buster. It's just seven long, slow, deep breaths, with eyes closed, focusing on your breathing. Use it to break up your days, such as morning, lunchtime, and evening.

Thoughts might pop in and out of your head. It doesn't mean you have to engage with them or resist them. Instead, just 'observe' them and even name them – 'there's a thought about 'x'. Then let them go and bring your attention back to your breath.

Try this short meditation, which adds a one-word mantra:

- Close your eyes.
- Take a long, slow, deep breath in through your nose, filling your lungs fully.
- Breathe out through your mouth, and mentally repeat the word 'calmer'.
- Do this seven times.

With regular practice, the mantra becomes associated with a calmer mental state. Something you can tap into, when you need it, as you just close your eyes, take a breath, and say 'calmer'.

Learning principle

Relaxation techniques are essential tools to control stress and anxiety and help you to perform at your best.[1]

Connections and overlaps

Carry on reading in order, choose one of the following or roll a dice:

1. Support (Chapter 12, pp. 95–102)
2. Wellbeing (Chapter 4, pp. 23–30)
3. Emotions (Chapter 8, pp. 59–66)
4. Motivation (Chapter 5, pp. 31–40)
5. Cognition (Chapter 6, pp. 41–49)
6. Assignments (Chapter 10, pp. 77–86)

B: Why does everything and everyone get on my nerves?

Q *Student life is really getting to me. Lately, I can't get through the day without something winding me up or getting on my nerves. Silly things can ruin an entire day. What's wrong with me and how can I turn things around?*

A Stress is not just about major life events; there's also a theory that it's a build-up of minor, daily hassles that wear us down. Things that usually wouldn't bother us cause us to 'fly off the handle' and ruin the day – the 'last straw'. A hassle in one part of our lives can have a knock-on effect on others. It's often not possible to work out what started the downward spiral, but a good place to start is sleep loss. It's a common cause of a bad mood and can colour everything else such as studying, social life, relationships, eating patterns, and so on. Added to this we buy into the myth that bad news comes in threes. So, one thing happens, and we look for the other two! By contrast, there is no standard multi-pack for good news!

Even if you haven't had a good night's sleep, the remedy lies in uplifting moments that can change the day for the better. At the end of each day, we do a mental balance sheet. If the hassles outweigh the uplifts, we figure, it's been a bad day. If the reverse is true, we call it a good day. In solution-focused coaching, a key principle is to control what we attend to. If we focus on problems, they get bigger and more vivid. Instead, we focus on solutions. In this case, the secret is, where possible, to predict, control, or avoid hassles and actively seek uplifts. Where you can't control a petty annoyance, you can control how you let it affect you.

With the hassles and uplifts approach you include stress-busting techniques in your daily routine. Make a list of your daily uplifts – little things that you can do. To work best these should be action-based, not food, drink, or ingesting stimulants. The idea is to get a psychological boost, so things like a walk in the park, a bit of exercise or social time such as sharing a joke with friends. It could also be giving someone else a boost with praise, a compliment or expressing thanks. There's also the go-to strategy of a few minutes of your breathing exercises. It's the easiest way to short-circuit the stress response. In short, make a habit of any activity, however small, that can help you take back control of your day and give yourself an uplift.

Learning principle

 To help to manage stress, balance out petty daily hassles with small uplifts.[2]

Connections and overlaps

 Carry on reading in order, choose one of the following (or roll a dice):

1. Wellbeing (Chapter 4, pp. 23–30)
2. Emotions (Chapter 8, pp. 59–66)
3. Support (Chapter 12, pp. 95–102)
4. Attitudes (Chapter 2, pp. 7–14)
5. Motivation (Chapter 5, pp. 31–40)
6. Techniques (Chapter 9, pp. 67–75)

C: Why do I have a love–hate relationship with stress?

Q *I leave everything to the last minute whether it is handing in essays, prep for presentations, or revising for exams. I think I need the pressure to get started. Then I have a few all-nighters and feel exhausted afterwards. This love–hate relationship with stress seems to be the only thing that motivates me. What else can I do?*

A You've worked out that stress is not necessarily a bad thing. Yes, it can help to get things moving, but too much has the opposite effect. When you leave everything to the last minute, you surf on a wave of urgency. However, it helps if this is not the only tactic you rely on. It's a question of balance.

It's useful to think of two types of stress. The harmful stuff – *distress* – is that mental state that overwhelms us so that we can't think clearly. The stuff that gives us an edge is *eustress*. There's a fine line between 'going for the burn' and 'burning out'. The key is to keep stress in the productive range. Another problem is that each time you use stress in this way you'll need to get closer and closer to the deadline to get the same rush. One of my colleagues routinely used this strategy and told me he was ready to start work on his project. 'When's the deadline?' I asked. 'Last Tuesday', he replied. That's when you know that things must change. No one performs at their best in times of panic. Even in crises, we need to take decisive action without 'losing our heads'.

When your motivation relies solely on external factors, you give away control. The solution is not startling or sexy. Create a routine, so you are not entirely at the mercy of the deadline. It's about how you manage time, day-by-day and week-by-week. The challenge is to commit to set tiny goals – things you can do even when you've got the flu. It's a tactic I use with coaching clients to build motivation. If the goal is small, you are less likely to resist it. Commit to 'going through the motions' so that the small goals become a habit. It need only take 20 or 30 minutes each day, or even just ten. Start with the easiest, most controllable bits of any goal. Doing some groundwork will help you to make more of the motivational rush from the deadline.

When the pressure of the deadline kicks in, it's vital you include stress-busting activities in your schedule. These help to keep stress in its 'enthusiastic' psyched-up range instead of burned-out 'overwhelm'.

Learning principle

Manage stress to keep it in its fruitful range and not tip over into 'a state of overwhelm'.[3]

Connections and overlaps

Carry on reading in order, choose one of the following or roll a dice:

1. Wellbeing (Chapter 4, pp. 23–30)
2. Cognition (Chapter 6, pp. 41–49)
3. Emotions (Chapter 8, pp. 59–66)
4. Attitudes (Chapter 2, pp. 7–14)
5. Revision (Chapter 11, pp. 87–94)
6. Assignments (Chapter 10, pp. 77–86)

Summary and what's next

With calmness comes clarity, so be pro-active and keep stress within its productive range. Make a habit of using relaxation techniques, so they become a skill you can call upon in times of stress and anxiety.

In the next section, we broaden the view to consider how your general wellbeing and lifestyle affect learning.

Checklist

Keep a track of which letters you've read.

A	**Read it**	☐
B	**Read it**	☐
C	**Read it**	☐

WELLBEING

How health factors impact on brain function, emotions, mental states, and learning

Clogged with yesterday's excess, the body drags the mind down with it.

> Quintus Horatius Flaccus (also known as Horace, 65 BCE–8 BCE), poet

[Please note: This information is not intended to replace professional advice tailored to your health and wellbeing needs. If in doubt, see your doctor.]

A: How can I clear my head and boost my mood?

Q *I sit on my butt for hours on end with my face stuck in a book or staring blankly at a screen until I can't take it anymore. I feel lousy most of the time. Trying to think is like wading through mud. What can I do to feel better and clear my head?*

A Lifestyle magazines tell us that 'sitting is the new smoking'. That's a bit over the top but sitting for too long does play havoc with posture. It numbs more than the buttocks. It can be mind-numbing too. Lengthy periods slumped at a desk can lower mood, which hinders learning. You don't need to rush out and buy a standing desk! 'Not sitting' can also mean walking, pacing, dancing or just stretching. In the words of James Brown, the Godfather of Soul, you just need to 'get up offa that thing'!

Studies show that students do better on academic tests on the days they take physical activity. Exercise steps up blood flow and gets oxygen to the brain – topside not backside! It revs up the cells in part of the brain critical for learning and memory – the *hippocampus*. Getting active can improve our ability to absorb new stuff and hold on to it. It also brings a near-instant, boost to mood. It lowers stress and anxiety, raises self-esteem, and can help to treat and prevent depression. But, there's no need to train for the Olympics. As with most things in psychology, moderation is key.

Shun the 'no-pain-no-gain' mantra. Aerobic activity – also called 'cardio' – is the most useful to improve mood and cognition. It's something you can do for more than a few minutes. Start with five and work up to 20. To boost energy, you need to work up a bit of a sweat and get the heart and blood pumping. This action delivers oxygen to your muscles and brain. Research shows that 20 minutes on an exercise bike works better to boost memory than those brain-training computer games. The key is finding an exercise you like. Cardio includes swimming, brisk walks, running, hiking, martial arts, and dancing. You could use rowers and cross-trainers at the gym. Work up to a gym class, such as aerobics or Zumba, which are also more sociable. Mix it up. Fit a variety of activities into your study routine. Just make sure it's not too late to hinder sleep. And, make sure you increase your water intake.

Whatever workout you choose to support your learning, be realistic – make it work for you.

Learning principle

 To break up your routine, engage your mind and boost your mood, move your body.[1]

Connections and overlaps

 Carry on reading in order, choose one of the following or roll a dice:

1. Stress (Chapter 3, pp. 15–21)
2. Emotions (Chapter 8, pp. 59–66)
3. Motivation (Chapter 5, pp. 31–40)
4. Cognition (Chapter 6, pp. 41–49)
5. Assignments (Chapter 10, pp. 77–86)
6. Revision (Chapter 11, pp. 87–94)

B: How can I get back in control of my body clock?

Q *My body clock has gone crazy. I'm up all hours, eating at weird times and my moods are all over the place. This doesn't help with a deadline for a group project with people who can't seem to focus either. Tempers are frayed! What can I do to get back in control?*

A One famous British politician claimed to get by on four hours sleep a night. 'They' didn't go down in history with the nickname 'joy bringer'. A high-up US politician also claims to have four hours sleep each night. Most of the world wish 'they' would have a couple more! Studies show that sleep loss can put you in a lousy mood, mess with your emotions, and impairs decision making.

Your body has an internal clock – known as a circadian rhythm. It's regulated by the *hypothalamus*, in the brain, and affected by daylight, darkness, and the hormone melatonin. Shift work, jet lag and a lack of routine tend to confuse these cycles. Tired people over-react! Sleep loss makes us grumpier, angrier, less friendly, and have less empathy. It's to do with the *amygdala* – a little almond-shaped part of your brain. It regulates how we deal with negative emotion. Tiredness also has a knock-on effect on appetite. It makes us more likely to snack on junk food. Sleep loss adversely affects attention and memory. It takes the shine off any success and can even lead to depression. It's enough to make you want to stay in bed!

However, there are simple steps to 'rise and shine'. First, work out how many hours sleep you need to be at your best. Rich, heavy meals eaten too late will keep you awake. You don't want your digestive system working overtime when it needs to rest. Late-night exercise can give you a surge of adrenaline you don't need – so workout earlier in the day. Caffeine and alcohol, too late in the day, can interfere with sleep patterns too. Staying up too late working, watching TV or using electronic devices means delays the time it takes for your brain to 'power down'. Also, if you have a power nap, do it before 3 p.m. and set a timer for no more than 30 minutes.

For long-term sleep troubles, review your routine. Make sure your bedroom is restful. Think Goldilocks. It needs to be cosy enough to sleep even with bears in the next room – hopefully, quiet bears. Is it all 'just right' for you? Are your mattress and pillows comfortable? Is the bedroom dark enough? Not too hot, not too cold? Control what you can.

At the next meeting of your group project, ask everyone how they slept. If everyone is tired, go easy on yourself and others, and keep the meeting brief. Set specific goals and assign tasks. Arrange another meeting soon, when hopefully you're all more rested.

Learning principle

Sleep helps you stay at the top of your game, keep things in perspective, and regulate your moods.[2]

Connections and overlaps

Carry on reading in order, choose one of the following or roll a dice:

1. Stress (Chapter 3, pp. 15–21)
2. Emotions (Chapter 8, pp. 59–66)
3. Support (Chapter 12, pp. 95–102)

C: What's the best energy drink on the market?

Q *I'm drinking a lot of coffee to keep me going but it's not working like it used to. Can you recommend any better energy boosting drinks?*

A Sometimes, we might need a 'pick-me-up', especially after a lack of sleep. But, it should be the exception, not the rule. Energy drinks usually contain caffeine, which in small doses can boost performance. However, too much has an adverse effect. It messes with your sleep patterns and adds to stress. The same for alcohol, especially close to bed-time.

The best energy drink is most likely water – after all, it makes up most of your body and brain. You don't need to guzzle down two litres of water a day. We are all physically different. It's just a guideline. Just don't get thirsty. Swap some of your tea, coffee, and fizzy drinks for water. Adopt the European habit of a glass of water with a coffee. Evidence on the effects of water on mental abilities is not clear-cut, but sports people are cautious. Some studies claim that as little as 1% to 3% dehydration can harm performance, such as attention, and short-term memory. Adopt the same caution.

Caffeine might help you to study longer periods, but if it puts you under stress, it means you won't absorb information as well. There's a difference between 'putting in the hours' and 'time well spent'. Always go for quality time rather than quantity.

Learning principle

 Drink water to maintain optimal cognitive functions.[3]

Connections and overlaps

 Carry on reading in order, choose one of the following or roll a dice:

1. Emotions (Chapter 8, pp. 59–66)
2. Stress (Chapter 3, pp. 15–21)
3. Cognition (Chapter 6, pp. 41–49)
4. Motivation (Chapter 5, pp. 31–40)
5. Assignments (Chapter 10, pp. 77–86)
6. Revision (Chapter 11, pp. 87–94)

D: What supplements boost brain power?

Q *When I'm revising for exams or have a deadline my diet tends to take a nosedive. Are there any effective supplements to boost brain power and memory?*

A Many supplements on the market claim to boost brain power. The most studied is gingko biloba, but the evidence is weak. And, even if it works, a few grams of an ancient tree are not likely to offset buckets of modern junk food.

Our relationship with food is complex. Food is fuel, but also a source of pleasure. We should treat our brains like luxury cars using premium fuel. Yet, more often, we treat them like 'old bangers' using any low-grade, quick-fix to keep us going. Also, we use food to control mood and get a temporary high. When tired or emotional, it's harder to resist the lure of fatty, sugary, or salty snacks. But junk food compounds the problem. Studies show a link between impaired brain function and lower moods, and sugary diets.

The food and mood link comes from *serotonin* in your body – the 'happy chemical'. It's a neurotransmitter that helps to regulate sleep, appetite, mood, pain, and sexual desire and function. It also helps with memory and learning. Some serotonin is made in the brain but mostly in the digestive tract, which is lined with millions of nerve cells – called neurons. It works with 'good' bacteria that protect the lining of your gut. These improve how well you absorb nutrients from food, and so affect energy levels and mood. It gives new meaning to the phrase 'gut reaction'.

Start by noting how various foods affect you, mainly refined sugars, and fats. Fad diets that suck the joy out of life are not the answer. Instead, look at traditional diets such as Mediterranean or Japanese. Use these as a basis for a 'brain friendly' approach. They have modest amounts of lean meat and dairy, and more fish and seafood. They also include more fruit, vegetables, more whole-grains, and fewer processed foods. Such diets are linked with a lower risk of depression compared with modern Western ones. Also, look into the 'good fat/bad fat' debate. A diet rich in omega-3 fatty acids supports efficient cognition and your brain's ability to adapt to change – *neuroplasticity*. By contrast, saturated fats get in the way. High-fat, processed foods might offer a lift the night before an exam, but what about the next day, when you need to be at your best?

There's also no need to adopt the no-carb craze or go gluten-free unless you have a diagnosed intolerance. Otherwise, it has no health benefits. Mainstream views hold that a complex organ like the brain needs complex carbs. So, switch to wholegrain types of bread and pasta and brown rice and see how these affect you.

It's said 'we are what we eat'. Or, as the computer adage GIGO puts it 'garbage in, garbage out'. It's hard to feel good about ourselves and be at our best with sugary, grease oozing from every pore! Overall, it takes just a few changes to your diet, to support your learning, rather than hinder it.

Learning principle

Get an edge by including more foods in your diet that raise mood and support cognitive performance.[4]

Connections and overlaps

 Carry on reading in order, choose one of the following or roll a dice:

1. Stress (Chapter 3, pp. 15–21)
2. Cognition (Chapter 6, pp. 41–49)
3. Assignments (Chapter 10, pp. 77–86)
4. Revision (Chapter 11, pp. 87–94)
5. Techniques (Chapter 9, pp. 67–75)
6. Motivation (Chapter 5, pp. 31–40)

Summary and what's next

General health and wellbeing – food, water, sleep, and exercise – impact on learning and mood. Changes in routine and lifestyle can give you an edge – even before you start to study.

In the next chapter we look at what drives you and how to stay on track – motivation.

Checklist

Keep a track of which letters you've read.

A Read it ☐
B Read it ☐
C Read it ☐
D Read it ☐

MOTIVATION

How to get started, how to manage time, and stay on track

What it lies in our power to do, it lies in our power not to do.
Aristotle (384 BCE–322 BCE),
philosopher and scientist

A: I get that Monday morning feeling every day!

Q *I rarely make 9 o'clock lectures despite my best intentions. I just seem to have that Monday morning feeling every day. Any tips for dragging my lazy ass out of bed in the morning?*

A We are motivated by many needs, which can be grouped into two driving forces – survival, and growth. These needs form a pyramid. At the base are physical needs such as sleep and rest, warmth, sex, food, drink, and exercise. At the next level up are safety and security needs, and then love and belonging needs.

Survival needs have priority over learning and growth needs. So, throw in a romantic liaison and breakfast, and it's a wonder we ever get out of bed! At the top of the pyramid – the apex – a long way up on a cold winter's day is the need to 'be the best you can be'.

To make the leap from 'base to apex ', don't buy into that 'Monday morning feeling' conceit. It will taint the day. Waking up on a Monday is far better than the alternative! Sleep has a major impact on mood, wellbeing, and cognitive performance. Are you getting enough? Next, ask yourself what is worth getting up for? What are you looking forward to that day? Pick three things. Porridge with coconut milk, a good coffee, and some social inter-action are usually enough for me. The secret is to pick at least one other basic survival need. Physical activity and fresh air are a good place to start.

To gently ease you into the day, I teach a breathing technique aptly called 'The Rise and Shine Breath'. It starts from the comfort of your bed, still lying down. It combines deep breathing with an early morning stretch. It'll get you out of bed and set you up for the day. Try it daily for a week (or even a month) to truly assess its effects. Read the steps a few times, before you start.

1. Begin with a long, slow deep breath in through you nose.
2. Bring your arms up to your shoulders and clench your fists, facing out, as if to lift weights – like a chest press.
3. Breathe out, through your mouth, making an 'aaaah' sound, like a sigh. As you do, push your arms towards the ceiling. Push as if there's resistance, like you're lifting a weigh. At full stretch, open your hands, and extend your fingers too.
4. Slowly pull your arms back to your shoulders with clenched fists. Again, pull down as with resistance and breathe in as before.
5. Do this seven times.
6. Now breathe in deeply (through your nose) and hold your breath for the count of ten seconds (if comfortable to do so).

7. Breath out forcefully through your mouth whilst pulling your stomach in.
8. Do three of these.
9. It's now time to sit up and repeat steps 1 to 4. Do seven breaths. Then repeat steps 6 to 8.
10. Finally, get out of bed and repeat steps 1 to 4, and 6 to 8 again.

You are now ready to face the world, or at least get to the bathroom, or to the kitchen to put the kettle on. With your basic needs met for the day, set three learning goals to meet your cognitive needs.

Learning principle

A breathing exercise and a good stretch is an energizing way to start the day.[1]

Connections and overlaps

Carry on reading in order, choose one of the following or roll a dice:

1. Stress (Chapter 3, pp. 15–21)
2. Wellbeing (Chapter 4, pp. 23–30)
3. Attitudes (Chapter 2, pp. 7–14)
4. Emotions (Chapter 8, pp. 59–66)
5. Support (Chapter 12, pp. 95–102)
6. Context (Chapter 7, pp. 51–57)

B: Always preparing to start but never starting

I can spend the entire day 'preparing' and end up doing nothing. I find loads of other things to do rather than studying. At least my underwear drawer is in rainbow-colour order. If I could just get my study timetable right, there would be no stopping me. Any tips?

A Yes, 'busy doing nothing'. We've all been there. Preparing to start but never actually starting – procrastination – is a sign of 'overwhelm'. If a job seems so big that we don't know where to start, we don't bother. Instead, we look for easy things we can manage – these are known as displacement activities. They are not essential or urgent, but we kid ourselves that 'at least I've done something today'. Usually, the stand-in tasks are simpler, easier to control, and yield results quicker. It's how we should manage our study goals

A popular evasion task is the 'perfect' study timetable. Draft after re-draft but never getting it 'quite right'. But it doesn't have to win any design awards! The key is to balance reflection with action. Thinking will only get you so far. Get the schedule good enough to get you started and refine it as you go. Here are a few things that will help:

- When do you work at your best? Are you a morning or afternoon person? Try out different start times.
- The brain likes routine. Treat your study plan like a day at the office.
- Do something physical to get you started. I begin every day with a brisk walk of ten to 15 minutes, no matter the weather. What would work for you?
- Use your favourite topics as a motivation to start the day and as a reward for studying the 'boring' stuff. Two half-hours of 'dull' earns you half an hour of the fun.
- Spending more time on the least preferred topics will improve your attitude to them.
- Timetable short intensive study sessions of about 30 minutes, with short breaks in between.
- Have a mid-morning coffee break and an afternoon tea break of about 15 minutes. And, don't forget that glass of water.
- Have a lunch break away from your study area. Don't have a heavy lunch. Keep it healthy.
- If your energy dips after lunch, go for a brief walk.

- Use a variety of learning activities to engage all your senses and maintain your interest.
- Begin each day with a few deep breaths and then review briefly, the previous day's material.
- End the day at a time that gives you chance to unwind ready to sleep.

Put these basic principles into practice, review, and adjust as you go. Your overall goal is to create a practical, realistic, plan that inspires action.

Learning principle

 A study time table is work-in-progress. It's a tool not a replacement for activity. Create a predictable routine.

Connections and overlaps

 Carry on reading in order, choose one of the following or roll a dice:

1. Emotions (Chapter 8, pp. 59–66)
2. Wellbeing (Chapter 4, pp. 23–30)
3. Stress (Chapter 3, pp. 15–21)
4. Attitudes (Chapter 2, pp. 7–14)
5. Cognition (Chapter 6, pp. 41–49)
6. Revision (Chapter 11, pp. 87–94)

C: How can I stop 'beating myself up'?

Q *Whenever I try to give myself a pep talk it usually ends up with me telling myself how useless I am. Most often I don't feel it's worth even bothering afterwards. Why do I do this and how can I stop?*

A Negative self-talk is a frequent problem I help clients overcome with coaching. The inner chatter is like a running commentary on our lives. It colours our view of ourselves and shapes our actions. Our self-talk is based on the rebukes and put-downs from parents, teachers, siblings, authority figures, and so on. Harsh words evoke strong emotions and stay with us longer. Then, we boost their impact as we turn them on ourselves using even crueller words. We repeat and rehearse these scripts until they become automatic. Most of the time we not aware of doing it.

Culturally, we applaud successful tyrants who belittle others on reality TV shows. We endorse the idea that 'a few home truths' will shock or shame us into doing better. But, it's lousy psychology. It often has the reverse effect. People thrive despite bullies, not because of them! Positive feedback is more valuable for growth.

Negative self-talk comes from a 'survive' mindset, based on fear. To shift towards a growth mindset, start by taking stock of the awful things you say to yourself. Write down your negative 'catchphrases' and your emotions at the time. Also, note how your feelings change. Do these put-downs shift you to a growth mindset or do they make you feel even worse? When we feel bad, we often go for a quick-fix to deal with the emotions, such as a piece of cake. If we feel overwhelmed, we might just go back to bed and not even try. Neither of these strategies will take you forward.

To begin to change your mood and mindset, take a few deep breaths and get physical, such as going for a walk. When you are calmer, it's easier to grasp the antidote to self-bullying, that is, to practise self-compassion. The truth is, if anyone spoke to you the way you'd talk to yourself, you'd never speak to them again! To challenge your self-talk, assume it's trying to be helpful. That is, trying to protect you from disappointment. Say to your inner-critic 'Thanks, but not helpful' and add 'once more with kindness'. Rephrase the put-down in a constructive, supportive way. Imagine saying it to someone else to boost their esteem rather than crush them. Then ask 'What changes do I need to make to refocus on my goals'? It takes a while to create new scripts. Overall, your challenge is to shift the accent of your self-talk from inner critic to inner coach.

Learning principle

Self-compassion is a better motivator than 'beating your-self up' and 'putting yourself down'.[2]

Connections and overlaps

Carry on reading in order, choose one of the following or roll a dice:

1. Emotions (Chapter 8, pp. 59–66)
2. Stress (Chapter 3, pp. 15–21)
3. Wellbeing (Chapter 4, pp. 23–30)
4. Support (Chapter 12, pp. 95–102)
5. Attitudes (Chapter 2, pp. 7–14)
6. Cognition (Chapter 6, pp. 41–49)

D: How can I keep sight of the big picture?

Q *Lately, studying has become a slog. When I haven't lost sight of the big picture, I'm worrying how I'll ever get there. What tricks do you have to quieten the doubts, help me focus, and get me moving?*

A In workshops, I use an exercise to help people to focus on the desired outcome for their goals. It's a motivation tactic used by top athletes to focus on the finish line. As with any technique, attitude is key. Ask 'how will it work?' rather than 'will it work?' It uses the acronym GRIP.

- G is for Goal – a statement of what you want to achieve, like 'get my certificate'.
- R is for Relax. Close your eyes and take a few deep breaths in through your nose and out through your mouth.
- I is for Image. Create a mental image of your desired outcome, such as the moment you get your

certificate. Imagine the sights, the sounds, and emotions. How will you be feeling? How big will your smile be? Imagine the people around congratulating you. Make the experience feel as real as possible. Don't worry how you got there. Just focus on the result, the happy ending, the finish line.

- P is for Persistence. Keep doing it. Make it part of your routine.

This process implants the idea that you've already made it. Once you give the brain a compelling end-point, it'll get to work in the background. It's like worrying except with a positive focus. Use it for any goals such as presentations, interviews, even first dates – anything where you fret about the outcome. The exercise brings calm, focus, and taps into your creative self. It's also an empowering way to start the day.

Learning principle

Support your goals and maintain your motivation with visualization exercises to keep your brain focused on the finishing line.[3]

Connections and overlaps

Carry on reading in order, choose one of the following or roll a dice:

1. Stress (Chapter 3, pp. 15–21)
2. Attitudes (Chapter 2, pp. 7–14)
3. Wellbeing (Chapter 4, pp. 23–30)
4. Emotions (Chapter 8, pp. 59–66)
5. Cognition (Chapter 6, pp. 41–49)
6. Revision (Chapter 11, pp. 87–94)

E: What can I do when there aren't enough hours in the day?

Q *There aren't enough hours in the day to write eight 2000-word essays in ten weeks, let alone all the reading. How am I supposed to cram it all in, and still have a life?*

A When we're stressed time seems to shrink. To counter this, the first step is to include stress-busting activities into your routine, such as breathing exercises or physical activity. Now reflect. Countless students have managed this goal, so in theory, you know it's possible. You just need to create a plan that works for you. Goal-setting is at the heart of coaching. You might have heard of SMART goals. That's Specific, Measurable, Achievable, Realistic, and Time-bound. Well, 'eight 2000-word essays in ten weeks' satisfies 'S, M and T'. From the deadlines, you also know in what order to tackle the essays. It's just the A and R to sort out.

Let's start with a working hypothesis. What if you treated studying like a job? That's eight hours a day for five days, with evenings and weekends off. In ten weeks, that's 400 hours, which is 50 hours per essay. Let's say, on average, people read at about 250 words per minute. Let's just take ten of those hours for reading. That means you could read 150,000 words – two books' worth. If you use an active reading technique and make notes while you read, you can plan the essay as you go. Would that be enough? If not, what adjustments would you make?

In one job, I had to interview potential students for a place on a part-time course. The main question I asked was 'What will you need to give up to be able to study on this course?' The most popular answer was 'give up soap operas'. Start by monitoring how you use your time. Where do you kill time? Also, when reading or writing, set a timer and see how much you achieve in 30 minutes. It will help to restore a realistic sense of time.

You now have the data to create a plan that's realistic and achievable. Make sure you build in relaxation time. You'll need to be flexible week-by-week and adjust your schedule when you need to. What is definite is that you do not have time to knock out eight good essays in the week before the deadline!

Learning principle

 When pressed for time, relax, account for your time and plan how to use it.[4]

Connections and overlaps

 Carry on reading in order, choose one of the following or roll a dice:

1. Stress (Chapter 3, pp. 15–21)
2. Revision (Chapter 11, pp. 87–94)
3. Wellbeing (Chapter 4, pp. 23–30)
4. Attitudes (Chapter 2, pp. 7–14)
5. Emotions (Chapter 8, pp. 59–66)
6. Support (Chapter 12, pp. 95–102)

Summary and what's next

Motivation is knowing what makes you tick. It's also having the skills and strategies to actively recreate the right conditions and routines to move forward and stay on track.

In the next chapter we look at cognition – how we can work smarter, not harder by using psychology rather than fighting it.

Checklist

Keep a track of which letters you've read.

A   **Read it** ☐
B   **Read it** ☐
C   **Read it** ☐
D   **Read it** ☐
E   **Read it** ☐

COGNITION

How to work smarter not harder – using human psychology rather than fighting it

The mind is not a vessel to be filled but a fire to be kindled.
Plutarch (46–120),
biographer and philosopher

A: Just give me learning theory in a nutshell

Q *I have an essay to write on learning theory in psychology and I just need the main points to get me started. The lectures just bore and bewilder. I don't want to read an encyclopaedia. Just give me the basics.*

A Learning is not a passive process where we just soak up information like a sponge. It's an active, sense-making process. However, it helps to have a frame on which to hang the detail.

And, as it happens, I use the acronym ACE to sum up a whole course in learning theory. It stands for Association, Consequence, and Example.

Learning by association means we make links between experiences, thoughts, concepts, facts, and figures. We start with simple bits of information and learn to build increasingly complex patterns. You might have heard about Ivan Pavlov's cruel experiments with dogs. Through repetition, the dogs learned to link a ringing bell with food. In the end, they drooled at the sound of the bell even when no food was given. It happens to us too. Just watching a TV cookery show causes our mouths to water. This process also occurs as we study – hopefully with less drool. We don't merely recall facts and figures. Our feelings about a subject become part of that subject.

Many students learn to associate exam revision with boredom and this attitude sets up resistance to learning. There are a few things you can do to offset this. To start with, go back to basics to clarify key terms. Also, vary your learning methods to make things more interesting. Next, think about how you link the content with real life. We remember better the stuff that means something to us. Also, think about how you might relate concepts and ideas between different topics. It's tempting to keep facts and figures in neat little boxes, but deeper learning is always about making connections.

Second, we learn from our experience of consequences. It shapes our behaviour as we tend to repeat actions that yield rewards and avoid those that don't. With feedback, we move ever closer towards a goal, such as learning a new skill. Using this approach, psychologists even taught pigeons to play table tennis! They did this by starting simply and then rewarding more and more complicated patterns of behaviour. Remember this next time you face a tough task. Just break it down into small goals and build on each success.

It's the same principle for feedback on essay grades. If something you do gets praise keep doing it, and if it loses marks stop it. It sounds obvious, but I've given some students the same coursework feedback for a row of essays. Some resist and repeat the same mistakes. It's not because they don't understand. When asked, they say they 'just don't see the point'. Two favourite 'serial sins' are poor referencing and not using the submission guidelines. When making your study plan use rewards to sustain motivation, such as breaks and time off. Also, use the subjects you love as rewards for studying the ones you're not so keen on.

Third, we learn vicariously, that is, by example. We observe others and learn from their successes and mistakes. We can also ask them questions. It's a quick way to work out if behaviours or actions are worth doing ourselves.

Learning is the process whereby relatively stable changes occur to our experience of associations and consequences based on our interactions with the world, through our senses. That's my definition. Now research yours.

Learning principle

Learning is an active, sense-making process. We learn by forming associations and considering consequences and we learn by example.[1]

Connections and overlaps

Carry on reading in order, choose one of the following or roll a dice:

1. Context (Chapter 7, pp. 51–57)
2. Techniques (Chapter 9, pp. 67–75)
3. Assignments (Chapter 10, pp. 77–86)
4. Revision (Chapter 11, pp. 87–94)
5. Stress (Chapter 3, pp. 15–21)
6. Wellbeing (Chapter 4, pp. 23–30)

B: What can I do if have the attention span of a goldfish?

Q *I get tired quickly and distracted too easily. What can I do if I have a very short attention span, like goldfish short?*

A Goldfish get a lot of bad press, and I've never seen a tired one. Dead yes; tired no. The whole attention thing is a bit of a myth. The study of goldfish has made a notable impact on our knowledge of memory processes. We are often told, in the age of the sound bite, that our attention spans are getting shorter. And looking back on old films and TV shows we see that drama programmes and news stories today are faster paced. But, it might be that content makers have just become better at grabbing our attention. Dramatic headlines based on research tell us that we have attention spans of just nine seconds, that's supposedly one second less than a goldfish! Smartphones get the blame. And yet, we can still get so gripped by something that we lose all sense of time. Attention is both a task and context dependent. It's easier to distract us during dull tasks, than it is for things that interest us. It's all about motivation. We habitually ignore the ticking of a clock clock, unless we can't get to sleep. Then, it sounds like a barn door banging in a storm!

We cannot attend to all the information that comes our way. Our brains and our heads would need to be huge! Instead, our attention is selective. It filters data based on personal relevance, interest, and novelty. For example, we can be in an intense debate in a social situation when someone across the room says our name, and it grabs our attention. It's because our names have a high priority for us. Our names go right to the core of who we are. And, if someone naked ran past you'd most likely break off the conversation, no matter how compelling.

We process information at varying levels of intensity. Some stuff grabs our attention, and so gets the full works. Other stuff gets a partial treatment and some things we barely process at all. All this affects how we learn and remember. There's also not complete agreement, in research, on the length of the human attention span.

A popular figure is an average of 30 minutes. It's a useful figure to work with.

It helps to think that each of our senses has its own power source. Relying too heavily on one sense depletes the power source, and we experience fatigue. The drop-off in power makes it harder to take in information. So, by the time we've sat there for three hours, not very much is going in at all. Yes, you need to put in the hours, but it's how you use the time that counts. Here's how.

First, it's harder to focus on anything we label boring – even more so when we add to the boredom! The challenge with learning is how you 'breathe life' into the content. Second, study in intense bursts with short breaks in between. In the breaks, do something physical. Get up and stretch or even do a few sit-ups. There's no reason why you can't tone your abs as you tone your mind! Third, create variety in your routine. Make it more interesting. Switch between different senses. Together these will help to prevent fatigue and help to make the information sticky!

Learning principle

Create variety in your routine, work in short intensive sessions with breaks to keep attention at optimal levels.[2]

Connections and overlaps

Carry on reading in order, choose one of the following or roll a dice:

1. Techniques (Chapter 9, pp. 67–75)
2. Revision (Chapter 11, pp. 87–94)
3. Attitudes (Chapter 2, pp. 7–14)
4. Assignments (Chapter 10, pp. 77–86)
5. Wellbeing (Chapter 4, pp. 23–30)
6. Motivation (Chapter 5, pp. 31–40)

C: What can I do if I have a memory like a sieve?

Q *What can I do when nothing seems to sink in? I can spend all day studying a topic. My notes should be seared into my brain, but the next day I can't remember a thing. I keep losing stuff too. I seem to spend half my life looking for my keys! What can I do to improve my memory?*

A In daily life, when we lose things, such as our keys or phone, usually, it's because we didn't pay attention to where we left them. We weren't mindful – our thoughts were elsewhere. That's when some bright spark asks, 'Where did you last see them?' Usually, this is not very helpful. If you knew that, you wouldn't be looking for them! To counter this, it helps to have a specific place for our keys, such as a hook or a tray.

When our memory fails us, we might think it's a recall problem. However, research shows that to make the material more memorable, we need to do more with it at the input stage. Information sinks in the deeper we process it. As a guiding thought, it's the difference between having acquaintances or making friends. You might wave to someone across the street, for years, and never learn very much about them at all. With a bit of small-talk, you get to know the basics. It's only through deep and meaningful conversations that you really get to know someone. Returning to your keys, you probably know them well enough to recognize them. But, can you recall any details or the key you use most? Can you describe the logo or brand name on it? Probably not.

To apply these principles to your studies, first, it helps to create routines and habits for studying. Context is a powerful memory aid. Second, work at doing more with the material at a deeper level. Rather than just trying to copy down every word in a lecture, aim to put the content into your own words. As well as linear notes try using spider–diagrams or Mind Maps. Use rhymes, mood boards, or anything to engage more senses. Guide your reading and study sessions with questions, then try to answer them. Discuss ideas with other people. When you explain things to others, you use different (and deeper) processes than trying to recall something you've memorized. Parrot-fashion learning takes a lot of time yet is still a surface approach. The rewards won't match the effort.

Yes, all this takes more time. However, in the short term, it deals with the boredom and improves our attitudes to studying. This shift means the information is more likely to sink in. It will also save a lot of stress further down the line. Otherwise, instead of revising for exams it's as though you need to learn everything from scratch. It's much better to get it right the first time.

Learning principle

 Information sticks, and is more memorable, when you engage with it at a deeper level.

Connections and overlaps

 Carry on reading in order, choose one of the following or roll a dice:

1. Techniques (Chapter 9, pp. 67–75)
2. Motivation (Chapter 5, pp. 31–40)
3. Revision (Chapter 11, pp. 87–94)
4. Wellbeing (Chapter 4, pp. 23–30)
5. Stress (Chapter 3, pp. 15–21)
6. Emotions (Chapter 8, pp. 59–66)

D: What if I just don't have a creative brain?

Q *I have a looming deadline on a project. It's supposed to be test of problem-solving ability and creative 'blue-sky' thinking. Yeah right! It's torture! Hours spent staring at a blank screen, totally frustrated. How can I get around the fact that I'm just not a right-brained, creative type?*

A First, let's dispel the myth. The right-brain/left-brain thing is a pop-psychology distortion of old research. It's what real neuroscientists call neuro-trash. So, just put it out of both hemispheres of your brain! Neuroscience has moved on quite a bit since the 1960s. And, forget about pink and blue brains too. Current research on the brain focuses on *neuroplasticity*, that is, the adaptability of the brain.

Stress puts us into a state of survival. It distorts our sense of time – it seems to speed up. In this state mental processes and emotional resources not vital for survival switch off. Everything becomes 'black and white, fight or flight'. While a bit of stress can help boost performance, too much makes problem-solving harder. Think about times when you have a word on the tip of your tongue but can't say it. Racking your brains, to force yourself to recall the word, doesn't work. You usually remember once the pressure is off. Relaxation helps creativity to thrive because we use all our cognitive abilities. We process information more efficiently and make new connections more easily.

Don't force things; let the brain 'do its thing'. It doesn't switch off; it's always working in the background. So, don't bombard your brain with data every waking moment. Give it – and yourself – a break! It seems contradictory, especially when we feel pressed for time. Yet, taking breaks speed things up. It helps you to work with your brain, rather than against it. In cognitive psychology, this time-out approach is called *incubation*. It really is like sitting on eggs to hatch them. There is no point shouting at them!

A change of attitude is always a good starting point. We think of a problem as a negative thing, but it's just something 'proposed for solution'. 'Pro' means to project forward, so think of it as a project. Begin by making the proposal as clear as you can. Write down all you know so far. Then add any other thoughts. Don't censor. Even a 'stupid' idea might lead you to a useful connection. Work, intensely, on the project but don't get frustrated. Then take a break such as a relaxation exercise, something physical, another task, or a glass of water. Your brain will stay on the case. Switch between intense bursts of work and short breaks to keep unhelpful stress at bay. It's usually on the breaks that we have the flashes of inspiration, the 'eureka moments'. And for harder problems, it might just help to sleep on it.

Learning principle

 To be more creative, the brain needs breaks.[3]

Connections and overlaps

 Carry on reading in order, choose one of the following or roll a dice:

1. Stress (Chapter 3, pp. 15–21)
2. Attitudes (Chapter 2, pp. 7–14)
3. Wellbeing (Chapter 4, pp. 23–30)
4. Emotions (Chapter 8, pp. 59–66)
5. Motivation (Chapter 5, pp. 31–40)
6. Revision (Chapter 11, pp. 87–94)

Summary and what's next

Don't do battle with your brain by trying to cram it full of unrelated facts and figures. Basic principles of psychology and learning theory can help you to work with your brain, not against it – how to work smarter not harder.

In the next chapter we look at the value of using context to frame our learning experiences and so make it easier to process information.

Checklist

Keep a track of which letters you've read.

A   Read it   ☐
B   Read it   ☐
C   Read it   ☐
D   Read it   ☐

CONTEXT

How where we learn affects how we learn

The world is presented in a kaleidoscope flux of impressions which have to be organized by our minds . . .

Benjamin Whorf (1897–1941),
linguist

A: How do I get a better grasp of study materials?

Q *I can read a whole novel and remember it all. But, with a textbook or a journal article by the time I've read the first page nothing has gone in. What can I do to get a better grasp of stuff?*

A With a novel, you know what to expect. It's likely you chose it because you're a fan of the author or the genre. When you read a review or judge the book by its cover, this offers the backdrop for reading. Research shows that having a context for new information helps us get a better grasp of its meaning and improves recall. In one experiment, participants read a short, vaguely worded passage about washing clothes. One group knew the topic from the start, a second group was told at the end, and a third wasn't told at all. When tested on recall and comprehension, the group that knew the topic from the start scored significantly better than the other groups.

Context helps us to link new material with our existing knowledge. With no framework, we must work harder to make sense of it. This extra effort can lead to errors in both understanding and recall. So, spend a little time to create the context for reading any text. Skim through it to get a feel for the layout. Read the chapter summaries and check out the glossary to clarify key terms. It's not a murder mystery. There are no spoilers. Skip to the conclusions. The same with journal articles. All this sets you up to tackle the big bit in the middle.

Learning principle

 Impose a context for new information. It aids understand-ing and recall.[1]

Connections and overlaps

 Carry on reading in order, choose one of the following or roll a dice:

1. Cognition (Chapter 6, pp. 41–49)
2. Revision (Chapter 11, pp. 87–94)
3. Attitudes (Chapter 2, pp. 7–14)
4. Wellbeing (Chapter 4, pp. 23–30)
5. Techniques (Chapter 9, pp. 67–75)
6. Stress (Chapter 3, pp. 15–21)

B: How can I find the best place to study?

Q *Where's the best place to study or revise for exams? I can't focus at the library and I end up falling asleep in my bedroom?*

A Where you study gets linked to what you study. So, try out a few places to get a space that supports learning for you. Bedrooms are often multi-use spaces, which can give the brain mixed messages. So, we can be wide awake when we should be sleeping. And, we're nodding off when we should be studying. Sleep loss can make you grumpy and gets in the way of learning. So, it's good to hear that your bedroom creates the right context for a snooze.

For studying, create a positive, and moderately comfortable setting to learn – a place you want to spend time and want to work. It shouldn't depart too much from exam conditions. Most likely, on the day, it'll be desks and chairs, not bean bags, a cosy bed, or a chaise longue. Lying on the bed to study can prompt sleep. So, if you have a desk and chair in your bedroom, use them. This habit is the cue that you mean business, and it's time to work.

If you use more than one study space, try to match the setting to the task. If it's a complex task, use a more formal place, with fewer distractions so you can focus. For a simpler or plodding task, a more vibrant place will help with motivation. In the exam, exploit the link between context and content. Don't hurry to start writing. If you try to force yourself to recall information, it can make it harder to remember. Instead, close your eyes and take a few deep breaths to calm your nerves. Now imagine your familiar study space. The context offers a memory cue, and the information you need should follow.

Learning principle

 The context in which you learn material can provide useful memory cues for recall.

Connections and overlaps

 Carry on reading in order, choose one of the following or roll a dice:

1. Attitude (Chapter 2, pp. 7–14)
2. Emotions (Chapter 8, pp. 59–66)
3. Motivation (Chapter 5, pp. 31–40)
4. Cognition (Chapter 6, pp. 41–49)
5. Stress (Chapter 3, pp. 15–21)
6. Wellbeing (Chapter 4, pp. 23–30)

C: Does music help with studying?

Q *I like to listen to music when I study but I'm not sure if it helps. I hate silence but get side-tracked when one of my favourite songs plays. Classical music is not my thing. It either annoys me or I fall asleep. What can I do to relieve the boredom and help me focus?*

A Music can have a profound effect on us at many levels. It can help to change our mood, boost energy, and improve cognitive performance. Research on *The Mozart Effect* finds that listening to classical music probably won't make us smarter. Music taste is a personal thing. And, other people's music is as bad as noise, even Mozart!

When you use sound to support learning, be flexible. It depends on the task. Cafés are now popular working places. Moderate levels of background noise can boost creativity. However, it's vital to pick your time. At peak times, the lively chatter might put you off. If the task is more complicated, both noise and music can have an adverse effect. So, if you're struggling to grasp new or 'difficult' material, noisy places or listening to music can make it worse. Silence is best.

Moderation is also key. The volume of music should be comfortable to you to support the main task. Just like in the movies, an excellent soundtrack supports the story not distracts from it. Otherwise, you'll put in a lot of hours but not get much done, except having something to hum! Music can also help with tedious tasks. But, there's a trade-off between speed and accuracy. Faster tempo music will help you work quicker, but it's more likely you'll make more mistakes. So, it's useful if you need to skim-read but not when you need to grasp finer meaning.

Research into music and 'speed learning' – chiefly for languages – is not conclusive but offers some insights on the type and tempo of the music. It suggests about 60 beats per minute – like a resting heartbeat – is the most helpful. When relaxed we can access a broader range of cognitive abilities. Not surprisingly, lots of the new-age meditation music has this tempo, although, bamboo flutes, wind chimes and whale song are not everyone's 'cup of herbal tea'. If classical music is your thing, the Largo movements in symphonies are about the right pace. Music can also reduce stress because it diverts us from things that disturb us. So, it helps to choose music that won't drive you to distraction! Equally, don't play all your favourites. Instead, use these for rewards in your breaks.

For my studies, I use music that doesn't evoke strong feelings for me such as baroque chamber music. I use it mainly to 'blank out' background noise. Also, I make playlists of 30 minutes to time my study sessions. I only use instrumental music as lyrics and vocals tend to divide attention. It's harder to get ideas into your head when joining in with 'Oops Upside Your Head'!

It takes trial and error to use music in a way that works for you but also sticks to the psychological principles. To be sure it does help and is not just a fun diversion, test yourself on what you've learned.

Learning principle

 If you use music to support learning, keep it in background and match it to the task.[2]

Connections and overlaps

Carry on reading in order, choose one of the following or roll a dice:

1. Motivation (Chapter 5, pp. 31–40)
2. Emotions (Chapter 8, pp. 59–66)
3. Stress (Chapter 3, pp. 15–21)
4. Cognition (Chapter 6, pp. 41–49)
5. Revision (Chapter 11, pp. 87–94)
6. Attitudes (Chapter 2, pp. 7–14)

D: The sweet smell of success

Q *What's the strangest technique you've used to aid learning?*

A The tip that students and coaching clients are quickest to dismiss is using their sense of smell. One client asked me 'Are you sure this is only something that works for you?' No! Smells are processed by the olfactory bulb that sends data from the nose to the brain. With the sense of smell, the brain is engaged in a different way to our other senses. For smell, it uses the same areas that handle higher level processes, such as emotion and memory.

When I began to use this tactic, it was about using all my senses to create a context for studying. I wore my favourite fragrance to revise for exams and during the exam. I don't rush to write. Instead, I spend a few moments to sniff my wrist with eyes closed and recall my study space. Over the years, this one smell has attained a powerfully positive association for me. Although the scent will be different for you, the process is the same.

Also, research can now point to fragrances that have helpful effects on learning and emotion. Lavender and ylang-ylang have a calming effect so are good to prepare for sleep. But, they won't aid memory. To remember, sniff rosemary or drink peppermint tea. Citrus smells can help to lift your mood and to get you started in the morning or overcome a dip in energy after lunch. However, there's no point using aromas you detest. So, experiment to find what works best for you.

Learning principle

 Use your sense of smell to add context to your study space, to aid memory and for a boost to energy and emotion.[3]

Connections and overlaps

 Carry on reading in order, choose one of the following or roll a dice:

1. Cognition (Chapter 6, pp. 41–49)
2. Emotions (Chapter 8, pp. 59–66)
3. Wellbeing (Chapter 4, pp. 23–30)
4. Revision (Chapter 11, pp. 87–94)
5. Stress (Chapter 3, pp. 15–21)
6. Motivation (Chapter 5, pp. 31–40)

Summary and what's next

Our pattern seeking brain works better when we set the scene. Context and environment create powerful memory cues for the better recall of information. The time spent giving a context for your studying and revision will lay the groundwork to combat exam stress.

In the next chapter we consider the impact of mood and emotions on studying.

Checklist

Keep track of which letters you've read.

A   **Read it** ☐
B   **Read it** ☐
C   **Read it** ☐
D   **Read it** ☐

€MOTIONS

How to deal with the emotional ups-and-downs of studying

I don't want to be at the mercy of my emotions. I want to use them, to enjoy them, and to dominate them.

Oscar Wilde (1854–1900),
playwright, poet, and author

A: What can I do if I'm never in the right mood to study?

Q *Studying goes okay once I'm in the mood. Trouble is, I'm rarely in the mood. What can I do to 'psych myself up'?*

A Who says you need to be in the mood? If the fire alarm went off right now, you wouldn't need to be in the mood to get the hell out of there. Many factors contribute to your mood, both physical and psychological. These factors include the attitude with which you approach something, how well you're sleeping, exercise, diet, and hydration. So, review these first. Also, recognize that sometimes, although we can make a task a bit more bearable, we might just need to 'bite the bullet' and get on with it. However, here's a short exercise to help you to 'psych yourself up', any time you need a boost.

First, decide what 'in the mood' feels like and the last time you experienced it. Perhaps pick an even more excited state, and name it. So, name it. Is it 'resourceful', 'energized', 'joyful', 'happy', 'in the mood' or 'in the zone'? If you've ever been in this mood, you can re-create it. If not, just imagine it. You don't have to be a great actor; just approach the exercise with a desire to make it work and exaggerate a little.

Try this exercise, once you've learned the steps:

1. Begin with your eyes closed and take ten long slow deep breaths in through your nose and out through your mouth.

2. Count down from ten to one on each out-breath. Imagine feeling more relaxed and going deeper each time.

3. Now think of a time when you experienced your chosen emotional state. Recall as much of the detail as you can. What were the sights, sounds and other sensations? What bodily sensations were there? Summon these feelings and emotions.

4. How real does it feel? Rate it on a scale from zero to ten, where zero equals 'not at all' and ten equals 'totally real'. What can you add to make it more real? Keep adding detail until it feels like an eight or above.

5. Next, add your trigger word or phrase (such as, 'let's go') to 'psych it up' even more. Repeat it over and over in your head with increasing emotion, really feel it in your body.

6. Clap your hands and get on with things.

As with any exercise, the effects intensify the more you practice.

Learning principle

 You don't have wait to be 'in the mood'; actively use your imagination to get in the mood![1]

Connections and overlaps

 Carry on reading in order, choose one of the following or roll a dice:

1. Motivation (Chapter 5, pp. 31–40)
2. Attitudes (Chapter 2, pp. 7–14)
3. Wellbeing (Chapter 4, pp. 23–30)
4. Stress (Chapter 3, pp. 15–21)
5. Context (Chapter 7, pp. 51–57)
6. Support (Chapter 12, pp. 95–102)

B: Can anyone change from a hopeless to hopeful outlook?

Q *Studying used to be an emotional rollercoaster of ups-and-downs. Lately it's just a sprawling crap-stream of hopelessness. It's like pushing a huge ball of dung up a hill and the dungball gets bigger and bigger. Is this outlook just part of my personality?*

A Wow! They are strong words and graphic images. Sorry to hear you're having a tough time of it. So, first up, if these feelings distress you, it's vital to get support. Have you told anyone, such as family or friends, how things are getting you down? It often helps to get another person's outlook. And, it can be easier to chat with someone you don't know. So, for some expert support try the advisors or counsellors at college or university. You could also visit your family doctor. Talking about it is the first step to getting over it.

Optimism and pessimism are not character traits. They are styles we use to explain events in our lives. We can unlearn a helpless, 'glass-half-empty' style and re-learn a hopeful, 'glass-half-full' line. Decades of research supports the idea that you can change an outlook of hopelessness. Although you could go it alone and learn to do it yourself, working with a counsellor or coach trained in Positive Psychology or solution-focused skills can speed things up.

Pessimistic styles and optimistic styles explain life events in opposite ways. After a negative outcome, the pessimist view makes it too personal, takes all the blame, and ignores context. Also, rather than a temporary glitch, it's seen as a lasting pattern. The helpless-style also goes beyond the evidence. It taints all aspects of life and ability. Whereas, a hopeful-style looks at context. It balances personal accountability with things beyond a person's control. It highlights the temporary nature of the outcome and what could change next time. Also, the result is only applied to a specific aspect of life.

For positive outcomes, there's a total switch in explanations between styles. The pessimist view writes off success as a fluke or luck, which won't last. Also, it confines the result to a specific area of life. By contrast, people using a hopeful-style own their part in the success. This approach emphasizes control and boosts self-esteem. Also, the optimistic view sees the outcome as something to repeat and extend to other areas of their life.

It's no surprise the pessimistic style is linked with depression. So, when you are aware of using the glass-half-empty accounts, stop yourself and review and opt for the glass-half-full versions. And, if in doubt, talk it out.

Learning principle

 Use hopeful explanations of life events over helpless ones. Choose 'boom and bloom' over 'doom and gloom'.[2]

Connections and overlaps

 Carry on reading in order, choose one of the following or roll a dice:

C: Is my addictive personality getting in the way of learning?

Q *How come every time I face the horrors of exam revision I develop an addiction to junk food and TV boxsets. Do I have an addictive personality?*

A Rather than an addiction, it's your way of coping. It's a quick fix to replace unpleasant motions with pleasant ones. As children, we learn that gifts of sweets or food help to 'heal' disappointment and sadness. As adults, we might soothe emotions with comfort eating or switch on the TV to help us switch off. It's a seductive, instant ploy to deal with the symptoms rather than the cause. It's called *emotion-focused coping*. It becomes ineffective, even counter-productive if it's the only tactic we ever use. So, we try to fix unhappiness about weight gain with more food. And, we'll try to fix the shock of the credit card bill with retail therapy, on the credit card! It's easy to see how relying on emotion-focused coping can look like an 'addictive personality'.

The alternative is *control-focused coping*. That's taking action to deal with what triggers the unpleasant emotions. It's not so quick, but its effects last longer than just dealing with symptoms. By far, the most common problem with studying is boredom. When you're bored, energy dips and time drags. Why would you be keen to spend lots of time doing something you feel bad about? The first step is to own the boredom, recognize you're adding to it, and then do something about it. Taking action is the quickest way to change attitudes. How will you make your study space more comfortable? Is it tidy? Is physical clutter adding to mental clutter? Also, mindless repetition is tiring. How can you create variety in your study routine? Work with short intensive blocks of study. Take breaks and do something physical to boost your energy. Make your TV boxsets a reward based on how much work you've done.

Overall, look for ways to take back control rather than mopping up the emotional aftermath.

Learning principle

 Use control-focused coping tactics to manage moods – go to the causes of issues rather than solely focusing on the symptoms.[3]

Connections and overlaps

 Carry on reading in order, choose one of the following or roll a dice:

1. Attitudes (Chapter 2, pp. 7–14)
2. Motivation (Chapter 5, pp. 31–40)
3. Wellbeing (Chapter 4, pp. 23–30)
4. Stress (Chapter 3, pp. 15–21)
5. Support (Chapter 12, pp. 95–102)
6. Cognition (Chapter 6, pp. 41–49)

D: What can I do if I've started to hate my course?

I'm worried I made a big mistake and am on the wrong course. I loved the first year. It was fun. I coped well and got good grades. The second year is a drag. I hate it and am tempted to jack it in and do something else. Trouble is I don't know what to do? Help!

It sounds like a case of the 'Year Two Blues'. The excitement of the first year has worn off and the challenges of the third year are a way off. Year Two can feel like a state of limbo. If you're not living on campus, this can add to the sense of feeling cut off.

There's a strong link between emotion and motivation. And, it helps to think of two types of motivation, external and internal. We have less control over outside incentives such as deadlines, money, and praise. Internal motivators are your goals and values. You have more control over these. To check if this course is still right for you, review the reasons you chose the course. Have they changed? Are your long-time goals the same? Do the syllabus and your goals still match? Review your long-term goals, regularly. It can help with other choices such as topics for presentations, module choice, and dissertations. When something's relevant and fascinates you, it stops being hard work. Instead, it puts you in a state of flow, where you become so engrossed you lose all sense of time.

Next, look for ways to re-connect with your course and other activities. How can you get more involved? What clubs, societies, other regular events are there? Also, look at stuff that might help to develop skills you can add to your CV (résumé) such as experience on the student newspaper. It could get you out and about meeting people. What about the staff–student committee? Okay, so you'll get loads of students bringing their problems to you, but that's the point: people will be coming to you. It's up to you to make something social of it. You'll also get to know the tutors on your course too, which is helpful for references.

There are lots of opportunities. You just need to seize them.

Learning principle

When feeling out of control, focus on the stuff you can control, however small.[4]

Connections and overlaps

Carry on reading, choose one of the following or roll a dice:

1. Attitudes (Chapter 2, pp. 7–14)
2. Stress (Chapter 3, pp. 15–21)
3. Wellbeing (Chapter 4, pp. 23–30)

Summary and what's next

Finding ways to gain control over emotion and mood will have a major impact on your motivation for studying. This chapter looked at the ways in which you can adopt a more control-focused approach to cope with the pressures of studying.

In the next chapter we consider practical study techniques.

Checklist

Keep a track of which letters you've read.

A **Read it** ☐
B **Read it** ☐
C **Read it** ☐
D **Read it** ☐

TECHNIQUES

How active learning strategies beat passive approaches

Tell me and I forget. Teach me and I remember. Involve me and I learn.

Benjamin Franklin (1705–1790),
politician and polymath

A: Do I need to bother taking notes in lectures?

Q *I struggle to take notes in lectures. How am I supposed to get down every word, when lecturers drone on without taking a breath? I'd have to be a superhero to get all. If I'm lucky, I end up with a page of scribble and doodles. Should I get a digital recorder? There's got to be an easier way. Help!*

A It's a mistaken belief that all you need to do is capture every word of a lecture, memorize it, and churn it out in an exam. It's a throwback to the school 'spoon-fed' approach. But, goals change. It might have been useful then, but at university it's not. Lectures don't replace reading. They set the scene and form the basis for your independent study. They're starting blocks, not finishing lines.

Always aim to engage with material actively to make deeper connections. This goal makes it harder for the information to be displaced in times of stress. For note-taking in a lecture go for quality, not quantity. Seek to get a feel for the topic and key terms and concepts. Instead of 'linear' notes, you might also try Mind Maps or spider-diagrams. Review your notes within 24 hours. Add what else you recall plus your own thoughts and questions. Underline what you don't fully grasp and find a source to explain it better. You might even find something to bring to tutorials. All this takes more effort, but it beats trying to make sense of things months later when revising for the exam. Then, you should aim to consolidate what you have already learned, not start from scratch.

With so many competing distractions, it's tempting to go for short-term gains when studying. Some colleges and universities record all lectures and probably this trend will continue. Although, it's debatable how useful this really is. For students with additional needs, this is vital. For others, it's used to cut down on the 'hassle' of learning. In the digital age, it's easier to capture information, but it's what you do with it that counts. Use technology to support deeper engagement with the learning material not replace it. The only thing that needs to be switched on in a lecture is you! Chances are you won't bother to review the recording until much later, if at all. It's best to get down the key points at the time and then spend time on additional research.

The most underused labour-saving study tactic is asking questions. In lectures, it can be scary, but it's a quick way to get information. Get into the habit of writing questions during lectures and ask them at the end. It could be you just ask them to explain something you didn't quite grasp the first time. Chances are, quite a few of your classmates didn't get it either. It's better to get clarification at the time than walk away confused. It'll save a lot of time down the line. As a student, I wasn't shy about asking questions, and as a teacher, I always encourage them.

How you deal with lectures and tutorials is good practice for dealing with meetings 'in the real world'. There's more to live and learning than 'digital capture'.

Learning principle

 Don't just try to capture every word in lectures, instead use them as a platform for learning, and putting things into your own words.[1]

Connections and overlaps

 Carry on reading in order, choose one of the following or roll a dice:

1. Assignments (Chapter 10, pp. 77–86)
2. Cognition (Chapter 6, pp. 41–49)
3. Revision (Chapter 11, pp. 87–94)
4. Support (Chapter 12, pp. 95–102)
5. Stress (Chapter 3, pp. 15–21)
6. Attitudes (Chapter 2, pp. 7–14)

B: What tips do you have for using highlighter pens?

Q *I've seen other students using highlighter pens on books but not sure how you decide what to highlight and what to leave out. Is there a system or rules that can help me to decide?*

A No! Bin them! The fad of daubing books in 'dayglo' highlighter creates the illusion of instant results but doesn't achieve very much at all. It's not learning. It's colouring in! When you come to revise the text, you have no idea why you selected some bits over others. The highlighted text could become more of a distraction. If you are committed to writing in books, do it in pencil. It's not so showy as highlighters but far more practical, and it's cheaper. You can go back and change your mind. You can erase old comments and add new ones. And, it doesn't spoil the books. You can then sell them on.

My favoured approach is to use a small notebook. I make notes as I read and then can add to them as thoughts occur to me. The brain always works in the background and can make connections at the oddest times. Carrying a notebook means I don't miss them. Writing things in my own words means I'm more fully engaged, cognitively. When I type up my notes, I add to them. There is less need for memory feats when you get involved with the material. Because the focus has been on 'sense-making', the knowledge is also less easily blocked or displaced by the stress of exams.

Many students also seem to have a passionate and costly affair with the photocopier! However, stockpiling papers that you'll never read is not learning, it's hoarding. You can't stroke them and learn by osmosis. Take a little time to skim through the article to gauge if it's really worth copying. Better still, just make your own notes from it and save your money, and the planet.

Putting in a little extra effort when learning will save you a lot of time, money, and stress when revising and during the exams.

Learning principle

 Ditch the passive highlighter pens and actively use a notebook and pencil instead to put things in your own words.

Connections and overlaps

 Carry on reading in order, choose one of the following or roll a dice:

1. Cognition (Chapter 6, pp. 41–49)
2. Revision (Chapter 11, pp. 87–94)
3. Assignments (Chapter 10, pp. 77–86)

4. Emotions (Chapter 8, pp. 59–66)
5. Motivation (Chapter 5, pp. 31–40)
6. Stress (Chapter 3, pp. 15–21)

C: What's the best way to memorize my presentation script?

Q *I need give to give a presentation but it's fair to say I'm not a natural. I've written it and am trying to remember it. It's not going well. As I rehearse, I stumble over the words, forget bits, and freeze. What can I do to make the information stick and not lose control of bodily functions on the day?*

A It's often reported that our two main fears are public speaking and death, and usually in that order! The biggest mistakes are imagining the worst and setting the bar too high. We see polished and charismatic speakers and feel we need to match that standard first time. We don't. For their first presentation, I tell my students and clients 'Aim for a pass. Anything else is ego!' Get the basics right before you get too 'showbiz'. Focus on how to get your information across in a modest, but effective way. This approach takes the pressure off.

Nerves and worrying cause us to imagine all the things that can go wrong. Also, when anxious we might stumble over our words. As the adrenaline kicks in, we speak faster to get it over with. With coaching clients for public speaking, the first thing we tackle is breathing and posture to aid relaxation. In stressful situations, we raise our shoulders. To counter the stress response, drop them. As anyone who's had singing or acting lessons will know: don't lock your knees. It can cause tension in the back and around the abdomen, which can limit the movement of the diaphragm and make breathing shallower – another sign of stress. So, unlock your knees and take deep breaths. Standing with legs shoulder-width apart, knees unlocked is also a more stable stance. Follow this routine as you prepare and use it on the day too.

Preparing for a presentation is not the same as writing an essay. Spoken and written language are different. Your main aim is to get it to sound right, not look right on the page. Otherwise, it will sound unnatural. You should be talking *to* them, *not at* them. Think of it more as a conversation and make eye contact. Don't just fixate on one person as if you're about to eat them. Remember to move your head to scan the room as you talk. In rehearsals speak out loud and go through the motions, don't just read through your notes. The same on the day. Reading from your notes or flashing up countless PowerPoint slides is not a presentation, it's karaoke! And to avoid producing slides that are really only prompts for you, use a 30-point font, to limit what you can put on them. Your primary support should be glancing at a few cards with bullet-point prompts.

A common worry is dealing with interruptions. Remember, it's your gig so tell your audience the format. I state from the outset that I'm going talk for so many minutes and take questions at the end. If people cut in, I ask them to 'hold that question', and I remind them I'll answer it at the end. If you do blank, it's a sign that stress is getting the better of you. It's also your job to put your audience at ease, so panicking and flapping won't help. Just pause and take a deep breath, collect your thoughts, find your place, and move on. If you need a moment, just say 'bear with me one moment'. Again, it's your gig. Audiences usually want you to do well. They'll 'bear with'.

It's a cliché but remember to smile! It will help with nerves plus you'll appear more enthusiastic, more likeable, and so connect better with the audience. Just turning up the corners of your mouth is all you need. In rehearsals, aim to 'up' your performance by about 10 per cent like you do when you have a surprise meeting with a colleague.

Finally, if you get a chance, check out the room in advance. It'll provide context for your rehearsals.

Learning principle

 Don't go for 'presentation karaoke' – instead, aim to connect with the audience.

Connections and overlaps

 Carry on reading in order, choose one of the following or roll a dice:

1. Cognition (Chapter 6, pp. 41–49)
2. Stress (Chapter 3, pp. 15–21)
3. Wellbeing (Chapter 4, pp. 23–30)
4. Assignments (Chapter 10, pp. 77–86)
5. Context (Chapter 7, pp. 51–57)
6. Emotions (Chapter 8, pp. 59–66)

D: Why doesn't information sink in from reading?

Q *I start with all good intentions of reading up on a topic to prepare for tutorials. But, after the first page, I realize I haven't got a clue what I've just read. I keep going back over the same stuff and end up giving up. What's wrong with me?*

A Once, my colleague ended a lecture telling students to read Chapter 14 of the textbook. One student asked 'And, which page in Chapter 14 is most important?' There's a difference between memory feats and understanding. Being able to 'throw up' page 69 in an exam isn't learning. Students are often instructed to 'read for a degree'. Usually, you're told what to read but often not *how* to read. Reading for entertainment and reading for education are different. Also, re-reading the same thing in the hope it will eventually make sense and stick is time-consuming, and not very effective. You can put in a lot of time with little to show for it.

For academic work use an active reading technique, such as the SQ3R method. It stands for Survey, Question, Read, Recite, Review.

- *Survey* – flick through the book chapter to get a feel for the layout and style. Scan the structure and subheadings. Look pictures and diagrams. Skim the introductory and concluding chapters. A quick way to get the gist of the content is to read the first and last lines of each paragraph. Also, bear this in mind when writing your essays.

- *Question* – what the chapter is trying to answer. Turn the title, headings, and subheadings into questions. Write them down. Ask how this information links to what you already know about the topic. These first two steps set up the context to fully process the material.
- *Read* – do this one section at a time, read to find the answers to your questions. Note all the information that has been emphasized such as bold and italics. Read slowly for difficult passages and make notes as you go.
- *Recite (and write)* – say out loud any key phrases which sum up the sections and answers your questions. Then, write them down in your own words. This practice takes more cognitive processing than repeating in your head.
- *Review* – what you've written for each section. This will give a list of bullet points for each chapter. Test yourself on these. For any you can't recall, go back, and re-read the section.

Yes, it's more effort than lying in a hammock, listlessly leafing through the latest celebrity autobiography; however, this structured approach works with the psychology of how we learn. It's the difference between putting in the time and doing what works.

Learning principle

 Use an active reading method to process the material right from the start.[2]

Connections and overlaps

 Carry on reading in order, choose one of the following or roll a dice:

1. Cognition (Chapter 6, pp. 41–49)
2. Context (Chapter 7, pp. 51–57)
3. Assignments (Chapter 10, pp. 77–86)
4. Wellbeing (Chapter 4, pp. 23–30)
5. Emotions (Chapter 8, pp. 59–66)
6. Revision (Chapter 11, pp. 87–94)

Summary and what's next

When you use active learning strategies and engage with the material at a deeper level you transform the knowledge. It becomes your knowledge rather than someone else's stuff you try to remember. When you aim meaningfulness and understanding the knowledge is less easily displaced by stress.

In the next chapter we look at how to manage the emotional ups and downs of studying.

Checklist

Keep a track of which letters you've read.

A   **Read it** ☐
B   **Read it** ☐
C   **Read it** ☐
D: **Read it** ☐

ASSIGNMENTS

How to get your point across in essays, presentations, and team work

Don't tell me the moon is shining; show me the glint of light on broken glass.

Anton Chekhov (1860–1904)
physician, writer and playwright

A: How can I improve my essay grades with minimal effort?

Q *Do you have any tips for shortcuts to improve my essay grades without having to put too much work in?*

A Get to the point, why don't you? However, this does go straight to the heart of the 'working smarter not harder' approach. Many students throw away valuable marks because they choose to ignore three basic principles that create a favourable first impression in an essay. These marks could make the difference between two grade bands.

First, do it by the book, don't 'do your own thing'. Read the submission guidelines for coursework. Follow the rules for font, margins, spacing, ink colour, and so on. 'Quirky' formats make you stand out for all the wrong reasons. They can be red flags for style over content or signs that you can't be bothered. It's good practice to act as if you were submitting a paper to an academic journal. The format is very specific.

Second, don't dismiss the value of a careful proofread and spellcheck. Grammar and spelling mistakes make it harder for the reader to follow your arguments. They also scream 'can't be bothered!' If you submit your first draft at the last minute, you'll see what you want to see and miss silly errors. Once you've 'slept on it', the faults are more likely to 'jump off the page'. A good tactic is to read your essay aloud. If you struggle to make sense of it, the tutor will too.

Third, learn the referencing system. No excuses. It's not an optional extra! It helps you to focus on supporting your arguments with evidence. It's also a sign you are a serious contender. A referencing system is a common language. It's like the bread-crumb trail in the fairy tale Hansel and Gretel. It tells the reader where you have been so that they can retrace your steps. It'll also help guard against plagiarism, that is, passing off other people's work as your own. Always write with the thought that your essay could be quoted by someone else.

These three principles are the gifts that keep giving. Once you've got them right, they will lift every essay, every time.

Learning principles

 Tend to the basics to create a good first impression in essays. Follow the submission guidelines, proofread, and get the references right.

Connections and overlaps

Carry on reading in order, choose one of the following or roll a dice:

1. Techniques (Chapter 9, pp. 67–75)
2. Context (Chapter 7, pp. 51–57)
3. Attitudes (Chapter 2, pp. 7–14)
4. Revision (Chapter 11, pp. 87–94)
5. Cognition (Chapter 6, pp. 41–49)
6. Motivation (Chapter 5, pp. 31–40)

B: My critical essay was too critical!

Q *I'm not happy with my essay grade. I put a lot of work into it and only got a pass and think it's unfair. It asked for a critical evaluation of a rubbish theory and I really did a hatchet job on it. The feedback said the essay wasn't balanced, with too much personal opinion and not enough references to primary sources, whatever they are. We are told to think for ourselves and then get marked down for it. How do I persuade the lecturer to up my grade?*

A It's always a let-down when the grade doesn't reflect the effort. But, before you charge off to see the lecturer, check out the marking criteria. Does your essay make the grade you think it deserves? Next, review the question. Did you answer it? Circle the keywords. Have you covered them? Also, key phrases in essay and exam questions give clues. They tell you what you need to do and how in-depth your essay should be. Words like 'describe', 'summarize', 'list' or 'outline' call for a less detailed approach. Words such as 'criticize', 'evaluate', and 'examine' call for a more in-depth approach. Terms such as 'compare and contrast' entail a mid-way line. As a rule, as you move forward in your academic career, expect to dig deeper.

Critical evaluation doesn't mean 'rip it to shreds' and calling it 'rubbish'. It's not tabloid journalism. Instead, you need to balance the theory's strengths with its weaknesses. Resist the urge to dive straight in with your take on it. Instead, begin with a neutral account, a description, of the theory. Next, deal with its favourable aspects before moving on to the weaknesses, and where improvements are needed. When asked to evaluate, it's not about your opinion. You offer conclusions based on the evidence you've given.

Also, a critical evaluation needs to use more than introductory textbooks. These only offer a general overview. And, they're out of date the moment they're in print! To advance your argument, use primary sources such as journal articles and new books. This tactic increases the chances of telling the reader something new. How many of your sources were less than five years old? Less than two? The past year? A lot can happen in a few years in research.

If you still want to see your lecturer, go with the aim of getting more feedback, and then act on it.

Learning principle

Read the marking criteria for essays and use the keywords in the essay title as a checklist of what to cover and how to approach it.

Connections and overlaps

Carry on reading in order, choose one of the following or roll a dice:

1. Techniques (Chapter 9, pp. 67–75)
2. Cognition (Chapter 6, pp. 41–49)
3. Revision (Chapter 11, pp. 87–94)
4. Context (Chapter 7, pp. 51–57)
5. Wellbeing (Chapter 4, pp. 23–30)
6. Stress (Chapter 3, pp. 15–21)

C: How do you survive group presentations?

Q *Help! I've got my first group presentation to give and I am dreading it. Team work last year was a nightmare. I started off planning a presentation and ended up plotting revenge!*

A Think of group presentations as character building! To survive, first recognize that some people will do more work than others. Your job is to practise your planning skills and communication skills and do your part. You can encourage others to do the same, but don't bet your life on it! And, don't let it get you down. Team-work situations really test our stress-busting routines. A few deep breaths might not be enough. So, check out the Buddhist 'Loving Kindness' meditation. It's great for boosting compassion and patience. You'll find it on the Internet.

At your first planning meeting, pick the topic, decide the order of the material and who's doing what. Allocate specific tasks, so everyone, in theory, knows what they are supposed to be doing for next time. Have some 'dress rehearsal' sessions and time the presentation.

It will help to alleviate nerves if you agree how to support each other on the day. So, when someone is speaking, the rest of the team should be actively listening. It reinforces to the audience what they should be doing. If someone is messing about in the background preparing their bit, it suggests what's being said is not important. Also, if you all pay attention, you can help out if your colleague freezes or falters.

Whatever happens on the day, it won't be life-threatening or life-changing. Keep calm and keep it in perspective. What really matters is that you behave with integrity, do your bit, and learn from the experience.

Learning principle

 In group presentations, practise your organization skills, behave with integrity, do you own bit and don't let it get to you.[1]

Connections and overlaps

 Carry on reading in order, choose one of the following or roll a dice:

1. Techniques (Chapter 9, pp. 67–75)
2. Stress (Chapter 3, pp. 15–21)
3. Emotions (Chapter 8, pp. 59–66)
4. Wellbeing (Chapter 4, pp. 23–30)
5. Support (Chapter 12, pp. 95–102)
6. Motivation (Chapter 5, pp. 31–40)

D: What's the best way to start an essay?

Q *I always struggle with the introduction to my essays. I'm getting a bit sick of writing 'In this essay I will discuss' but I can't think what else to write. And, I'm not too sure about what goes in the conclusions either. Any tips? Is there a template?*

A My pet hate is the essay that announces it's an essay – the standard 'This essay will discuss' line. Tell me something I don't know! It's unlikely that your lecturer will insist on this for an opening line but, if in doubt, ask. I urge writers to consider their readers. The person who marks your coursework reads a lot of stuff. Use the first 50 words to grab their attention and set the scene. It'll make their job easier and make your essay stand out. But don't write solely for the tutor.

Check out how professional authors write introductions in academic book chapters and journal articles. With my students and coaching clients, I use a couple of analogies. First, watch the news on TV. It starts with 'what's coming up' so you can tell in moments if it's worth watching. Second, imagine you must spend a cold night on a park bench. You find an essay that starts 'This essay will discuss . . .'. Chances are it'll go down your pants for extra insulation. But if the essay sparks your curiosity perhaps you'll read it to take your mind off the cold.

Begin your essay with a hook – like a quotation or a statistic. Can you link it to a topical news story? It only needs to be a few lines. Include a paraphrased version of the essay question. The reader should be able to tell what it's about without seeing the question. Then move on to tell the reader what to expect in the main body of the essay. This context helps your reader process the information.

You might have heard the rule for an essay in three parts. In the introduction, you tell them what you're going to tell them. In the main body, you tell them. In the conclusions, you tell them what you've told them. The main body is where you present all your evidence. It helps to think of each paragraph in the main body as mini-essays. Start with a sentence to introduce it, and end with a concluding sentence that also links to the next paragraph. Lead the reader through your argument. The conclusion section is a mirror image of the introduction. It's not the place to offer new evidence. It needs an opening line, the essay question paraphrased again and, not surprisingly, conclusions based on the evidence you've given.

Once you've got the basics right, there are plenty of Internet sites to help you to fine-tune your writing style.

Learning principle

In essays, grab the reader's attention in the first 50 words rather than telling them it's an essay. And, write as if it's more than just an essay!

Connections and overlaps

Carry on reading in order, choose one of the following or roll a dice:

1. Techniques (Chapter 9, pp. 67–75)
2. Cognition (Chapter 6, pp. 41–49)
3. Revision (Chapter 11, pp. 87–94)
4. Context (Chapter 7, pp. 51–57)
5. Attitudes (Chapter 2, pp. 7–14)
6. Motivation (Chapter 5, pp. 31–40)

E: Help! My lecturer is an idiot!

Q *I always struggle to stick to the word length in essays and often go well over. I've been marked down for it a couple of times, which doesn't seem fair to me. I did more work. The lecturer says my essays are wordy and rambling. He should talk! He's also asked whether it's all my own work. Cheek! It's not my fault he's got a limited vocabulary and is not so widely read. Any advice on writing for an idiot?*

A Wow! There's a thing called the *Dunning–Kruger effect*. Check it out! Put simply, 'you don't know what you don't know'. It's vital to have the right attitude to studying. It can make life much easier. So, what if you give your lecturer the benefit of the doubt?

There's a joke about a man who writes a letter and ends with an apology that the letter is too long, as he didn't have time to write a shorter one. Good essays are as much about what we leave out as what we put in.

First, check the submission guidelines and marking criteria. Has your lecturer followed these? Do the instructions mention you will be marked down for going over or under the word length? It's usually plus or minus 10 per cent. Next, go through your essay paragraph by paragraph and ask, 'does this answer the question?' One of the most popular tips to improve writing is 'kill your darlings'. It refers to those pet pieces of writing that we love and can't bear to part with, even though they don't really fit. Most writers are guilty of it. Rather than trying to shoehorn them in, just be ruthless. Cut them out and save them for another piece.

To edit your essay, go old school and print off a copy. When you lay out the pages side by side, it's easier to spot what to cut. As part of my process, I select one paragraph and cut and paste it into another document, which I name 'scratchpad'. I then edit it, and once I'm happy, I paste it back into the original document. I repeat the process for each paragraph. It really helps to cut out the waffle.

Don't write for your tutor. Write for a well-informed 14-year-old. That should hit the right tone and reading age. To make it more readable use sentences no longer than 20 words. And, write in plain English. Don't 'promulgate your esoteric cogitations' when it's enough to 'make known your deepest thoughts'. Big words can be red flags. If used incorrectly, it can signal you don't understand what you've written. They also suggest a 'cut and paste job', especially when there are also variations in style. There's software now to detect that sort of thing! So, use your own words. However, remember if it's someone else's idea, you still need to reference it.

These pointers are magic! Not only will they improve your essays, they'll transform your lacklustre lecturer into a person of discernment!

Learning principle

Use marking criteria and use the essay question as a guide for editing.

Connections and overlaps

Carry on reading in order, choose one of the following or roll a dice:

1. Techniques (Chapter 9, pp. 67–75)
2. Cognition (Chapter 6, pp. 41–49)
3. Attitudes (Chapter 2, pp. 7–14)
4. Emotions (Chapter 8, pp. 59–66)
5. Stress (Chapter 3, pp. 15–21)
6. Support (Chapter 12, pp. 95–102)

Summary and what's next

Essays and coursework can be markedly improved by attending to the basics such as reading the submission guidelines and marking criteria. This also includes applying the psychology of first impressions.

In the next chapter we look at revision tips for doing well in exams.

Checklist

Keep a track of which letters you've read.

A	Read it	☐
B	Read it	☐
C	Read it	☐
D	Read it	☐
E	Read it	☐

REVISION

How to prepare for exams, and make knowledge stick

The two enemies of human happiness are pain and boredom.
Arthur Schopenhauer (1788–1860),
philosopher

A: What's your best tip for exam revision?

Q *I dread revising for exams. Hours sitting rooted to the spot, boring the knowledge into brain, reading and reading my notes. What could I do that's a bit more dynamic?*

A My favourite technique, I call the *fantasy lecture*. It might seem a little 'off-the-wall' but it's fun, and it really makes the information stick. It's based on the idea that it's easier to tell a story than it is to memorize a list of facts. So, prepare to give a 20-minute talk to an imaginary audience – well, your empty room. Start by progressively condensing your notes. Write out each updated version and speak the words aloud too. Cut them down to a list of bullet points to use as prompts for your talk.

When you're ready, take a few deep breaths, set a timer for 20 minutes, stand up and address the room on your chosen topic. The idea is that you talk for the whole time without a break. You can glance at your bullet points, but you should carry on as though it were a real talk. Timing the talk creates a little stress, which boosts performance. As you speak, your brain fills in the gaps to connect the points using your own words. These links have more to do with understanding than mere memory feats. They're your words, so they're easier to remember. Clearly, this is an effective way to prepare for real presentations too. You could then try it out in your study groups. Some find it useful to record the lecture, play it back and make a note of the new thoughts and insights. I usually pace about 'self-help guru style' for my mock talk to get some much-needed exercise to counteract too much sitting. However, don't pace about too much on the day. It can be distracting to your audience, unless you're at an 8000 seat arena.

The technique actively consolidates the knowledge. It might feel strange at first, but it works, and it's much better than passively reading and re-reading through your notes until your eyes glaze over.

Learning principle

 Give short, timed talks on topics to help create new connections to the material.[1]

Connections and overlaps

 Carry on reading in order, choose one of the following or roll a dice:

1. Cognition (Chapter 6, pp. 41–49)
2. Techniques (Chapter 9, pp. 67–75)
3. Assignments (Chapter 10, pp. 77–86)
4. Context (Chapter 7, pp. 51–57)
5. Wellbeing (Chapter 4, pp. 23–30)
6. Stress (Chapter 3, pp. 15–21)

B: How can I stop myself from dying of boredom while revising?

Q *I dread revising for exams. It must be the most boring thing ever! Just the prospect of it and the life drains from my body. What can I do to relieve the ennui?*

A Revision for exams is a lot less boring when you stop adding to the boredom. First step? Ennui? Ditch the melodrama! It's not a fatal situation. Merely saying so reinforces a negative attitude that acts as a barrier to learning. At the theatre, we know it's make-believe, but we suspend our disbelief and get wrapped up in the moment. So, put your energy into making revision time more interesting. Start by getting the scenery right – a motivating study space. It will help create a more positive attitude and context for learning. It needs to be somewhere comfortable but also matches exam conditions as closely as possible. So, if it's your bedroom, use a desk and chair instead of lying on the bed.

Next, consider which activity you find the most boring. What else might you do? A favourite revision technique is reading and re-reading lecture notes. It's a very passive activity and uses only surface processing. It might help you to recognize your notes in a police line-up, but not enough to describe them in detail to a sketch artist! Instead, use an active reading technique that involves reading, writing, asking questions, and testing yourself.

Mindless repetition of the same task is a drain on energy levels. Different senses use different parts of the brain. So, mix it up. When studying, a change is as good as a rest. Switching between several types of activity helps to maintain full attention and makes the information more likely to sink in. Practising sample questions means you think about how to apply the knowledge you've learned. This process creates new connections. Using spider-diagrams, Mind Maps , making up rhymes and acronyms all require deeper processing. It might seem like a lot more effort. But, it's far less tiring than 'boring yourself to death', and it's less likely that the information will be displaced in by stress of the exam room.

As you revise, you can also prepare to guard against stress. Start each revision session by closing your eyes and taking a few, long slow deep breaths. This simple exercise will lower your stress levels and put you in a better state for taking in information. If you practise this routinely, it will make it more effective when you use it during the exam. Looking after the basics of sleep, hydration, exercise, and diet will also have a beneficial effect on mood and learning ability.

How you structure your revision day also impacts on mood and how effectively you process information. Ideally, revise for brief, intensive sessions of 30 minutes, with short breaks in between. During your breaks, get up, stretch, or even do a few sit-ups. There's no reason why you can't pass exams and have great abs. Ideally, treat the revision day like a day at the office. Have mid-morning and mid-afternoon breaks of about 15 minutes each. Have a proper lunch break away from your study space. The breaks help to boost attention and give the brain space to digest information. If you revise during the evening, make sure you leave time to unwind before you go to bed. At the start of each day, review the stuff from the previous day. It will consolidate the material and help to build connections.

Taking time to add structure, variety, having well-timed breaks and an emphasis on active learning and deeper processing will keep you in the peak mood and mindset to retain information and keep at bay your *ennui* – or boredom as we call it in the real world.

Learning principle

If your study routine is boring, take responsibility and make it interesting.[2]

Connections and overlaps

Carry on reading in order, choose one of the following or roll a dice:

1. Emotions (Chapter 8, pp. 59–66)
2. Stress (Chapter 3, pp. 15–21)
3. Motivation (Chapter 5, pp. 31–40)

C: There's never enough time in exams

Q *I always run out of time in exams. I spent a lot of time on the question I can answer, which then doesn't leave much time for anything else. Although I can write some brilliant answers, I'm usually disappointed with the grade. Any tips for better time keeping?*

A It's a common mistake to get so excited when we see a question in the exam on your pet topic. Our love affairs with some subjects started at the learning stage and are reinforced at the revision stage. Put simply, we spend more time on stuff we like. It can limit our options. In the exam, it's tempting to get carried away and hope that we will astound the examiner with the perfect answer to one question. It won't be enough. Sadly, if you answer one item out of three, you can only get 33-and-one-third, even if it's perfect.

In the exam, you need to answer a certain number of questions in an allotted time. So, allow five minutes to read the questions and at least ten to 15 minutes to check and correct your answers at the end. Divide the remaining time between the number of questions. All exam answers follow the law of diminishing returns. Basically, you write more and more for less and less. You get the bulk of the marks early on. In other words, invest in the cake, not in the icing.

To maximize your time, begin by closing your eyes and taking a few long, slow deep breaths. It will take stress levels down and counter the distorted perception of time. Now read the questions and underline any keywords.

Start with your favourite, take another deep breath, and map out a rough plan for your answer. Then write your answer but stick to the allotted time. As time draws to an end for this question, use bullet points instead of writing full paragraphs. Then, leave space to come back to it if time allows. Move on to the next question and repeat the process. If you exhaust all you can write on your least favourites, you get to go back to your pet topic.

If you still have time left out, check and recheck, especially for illegible handwriting. Make it clear. Help the examiner!

Finally, there are no extra marks for leaving the exam early. Just 'what ifs'.

Learning principle

 Always plan to answer the number of questions required in an exam.[3]

Connections and overlaps

 Carry on reading in order, choose one of the following or roll a dice:

1. Motivation (Chapter 5, pp. 31–40)
2. Techniques (Chapter 9, pp. 67–75)
3. Assignments (Chapter 10, pp. 77–86)
4. Stress (Chapter 3, pp. 15–21)
5. Emotions (Chapter 8, pp. 59–66)
6. Wellbeing (Chapter 4, pp. 23–30)

D: What revision tips do you have for a wanton slacker?

Q *I've got three weeks to go before my first exam. What revision techniques do you advise to counteract a year of slacking?*

A I suspect you kind of know the answer to this question already. Although you can't make up for lost time, you can make the most of what you have left. To achieve your goal, you'll need an action plan for studying and general wellbeing. It's pointless working a punishing schedule that will leave you exhausted for the exam. To get yourself into a productive mindset, it will help to 'role play' the different skills you'll need. So, organize like a wedding planner, train like an athlete, keep track like an accountant and think like a psychologist.

Treat revision like a job. That means you get up early and put in a full 'day at the office' and stick to regular hours. Start with a review of what information you have, identify the gaps and how you can fill them. Also, identify any theory that crosses over into more than one of your subjects. In psychology, it's schema theory. You can bring it into almost anything. Look through past exam papers to spot recurring themes and questions. Sometimes tutors will give hints in revision sessions. Use them.

Looking after your health will help your brain to be in its most receptive state to soak up the information better. Active and more in-depth learning strategies engage all your senses and are more productive. In short, they help stuff to stick quicker and for longer.

And, just because you can get through with a last-minute strategy, doesn't mean you should make a habit of it. To reach your potential, you need to put in the work consistently over time.

Learning principle

 Study consistently throughout the year, rather than leaving things to the last minute. For a complete course on how to study more efficiently, sit down, relax, and read this book. It will only take you an afternoon!

Connections and overlaps

 Carry on reading in order, choose one of the following or roll a dice:

1. Motivation (Chapter 5, pp. 31–40)
2. Wellbeing (Chapter 4, pp. 23–30)
3. Cognition (Chapter 6, pp. 41–49)
4. Emotions (Chapter 8, pp. 59–66)
5. Stress (Chapter 3, pp. 15–21)
6. Techniques (Chapter 9, pp. 67–75)

Summary and what's next

Consolidate your learning through active revision strategies. At the very least they will ease the pain of boredom. You might even enjoy revising! Most importantly, active strategies will make the information more sticky.

In the final chapter (if you're reading cover-to-cover) we look at what support you might need as a student, who to ask and how to ask for it.

Checklist

Keep a track of which letters you've read.

A   Read it ☐
B   Read it ☐
C   Read it ☐
D   Read it ☐

SUPPORT

How to help other people to help you

Help me during the flood, and I will help you during the drought.
African proverb

[*Please note*: This is for general information only and does not replace professional advice for your specific emotional and mental health needs. If in doubt, seek professional support.]

A: University is not as exciting as on TV!

Q *University is not what I'd hoped for. Most lectures go right over my head. And, it's not like it is on TV. I know it wasn't going to be lively chats over sherry in the tutor's parlour. But, I didn't expect 'Dawn of the Living Dead'. In tutorials, everyone sits in silence. I don't speak up because I don't want to look stupid. I think I need a one-to-one tutor. If I ask my parents, they'll know I'm not coping. How can I find a good tutor who won't cost the earth?*

A Before you spend any money, how can you make the most of what you have? In my work as an academic coach, most often we look at how a change in attitude boosts confidence. Worrying about what you think others think about you is like trying to read minds. It's a waste of energy. At the next tutorial look around the room. You'll see lots of furrowed brows and glazed eyes. A room full of people who'd rather help to create a tortured silence than break it. All waiting for someone else to speak up. Be the one! You don't need to think of a smart question. Just say 'I didn't quite grasp that could you explain it again please?' Others are more likely to be grateful and relieved. People might even approach you afterwards and you might even start your own study group.

If the world of learning is not what you'd hope for, nudge it in the right direction! It brings a topic to life when you exchange thoughts and ideas with others. And, the surest way to test if you know something is to explain it to someone else. It will deepen your understanding. I used this approach at university and did much better than people who tried to keep it all to themselves. Also, remember that lecturers and tutors are there to help. Speak up in tutorials, ask questions in lectures, or book a slot to see tutors in between times. Ask other students. All this can make lighter work of studying. Be a sociable learner.

Learning principle

 Be brave. Question. Talk. Explain.

Connections and overlaps

 Carry on reading in order, choose one of the following or roll a dice:

1. Attitudes (Chapter 2, pp. 7–14)
2. Emotions (Chapter 8, pp. 59–66)
3. Motivation (Chapter 5, pp. 31–40)
4. Stress (Chapter 3, pp. 15–21)
5. Cognition (Chapter 6, pp. 41–49)
6. Assignments (Chapter 10, pp. 77–86)

B: My social life and study life clash!

Q *Every time I plan to do extra reading my friends call or drop by. My best intentions disappear, and we hang out and get wasted. The next morning, I feel crap and unprepared. I'm also angry with them but more angry with myself. But, I'm not sure how to change things. Help!*

A It might sound dull, but this is all down to ground rules, balance, and discipline. Learning and studying shouldn't take over everything. You haven't joined a cult. There are times when you must work but also times when you should play. It's just a matter of when you play. It's best *not* to 'get wasted' when you have an exam or a presentation the next day. No one performs at their best with a hangover. However, don't feel pressured into drinking or taking drugs either. Some students will experiment, but it's not compulsory.

Student life is about juggling competing demands to get a work–life balance. Conflicts will arise when you aren't clear with yourself. So, the first step is to decide what 'balance' feels like to you. The next step is to let others know. In the initial stages, put things in the diary such as 'extra reading night' and let others know. It will take a while for people to learn your routine and it's up to you to reinforce it. However, build in a little flexibility. Sometimes you will need to 'stick to your guns' and at others you can 'let things go'. If it's your best friend's birthday and you haven't got an exam the next day, you can relax. If you have an exam, you'll need to bargain and compromise. Overall, aim to stick to your plan 80 per cent of the time.

Socializing is a crucial part of student life, so it might sound boring to talk about routines. However, always keep sight of the main reasons for studying. It's to 'open doors' not prop up bars.

Learning principle

 Create a routine that sets clear boundaries and balances study time with down-time.

Connections and overlaps

 Carry on reading in order, choose one of the following or roll a dice:

1. Attitudes (Chapter 2, pp. 7–14)
2. Motivation (Chapter 5, pp. 31–40)
3. Stress (Chapter 3, pp. 15–21)
4. Cognition (Chapter 6, pp. 41–49)
5. Techniques (Chapter 9, pp. 67–75)
6. Emotions (Chapter 8, pp. 59–66)

C: I'm tired of pretending to cope

Q *Nothing prepared me for the final year at university. When I'm not in a state of panic, I feel frozen. I'm also sick and tired of pretending to cope when I'm not. I know it's only studying. There are lots of people in the world who have real problems. I just want to get on a bus and not come back! Help.*

A Just because some people might have it worse, doesn't mean that your problems aren't important. Often, it's seen as a sign of weakness to ask for help. It's not. Top athletes have a team to support them. The difference is, they don't have to ask. It's just accepted that an athlete needs help to win medals. It's also the basis for life coaching – 'two heads are better than one'. When stressed we go into 'survival mode'. It becomes all fight and flight – survive rather than thrive. A coach shares the burden by helping you to organize your thoughts. As you relax, you free up your creative side.

You don't have to go it alone. There are many places to go to start conversations to help you move forward. Begin with friends and family. Talk to one of your tutors. Universities and colleges usually have support services too. A quick online search will yield websites aimed at student support or life in general, including telephone helplines. If things feel overwhelming, book an appointment to speak to your doctor.

Pretending to cope is such a waste of energy. Bite the bullet, get some support, and use the energy to move forward.

Learning principle

Part of the learning process is knowing when to ask for support. The sooner you ask, the sooner you can get back on track.[1]

Connections and overlaps

Carry on reading in order, choose one of the following or roll a dice:

1. Stress (Chapter 3, pp. 15–21)
2. Wellbeing (Chapter 4, pp. 23–30)
3. Emotions (Chapter 8, pp. 59–66)
4. Motivation (Chapter 5, pp. 31–40)
5. Attitudes (Chapter 2, pp. 7–14)
6. Techniques (Chapter 9, pp. 67–75)

D: My parents drive me up the wall

Q *My parents and family drive me up the wall! I know they think they're helping but asking me 'how's it going' six billion times a day really isn't! And the minute I have a break, they 'joke' that I'm not going to pass exams standing in the kitchen. I'm one step away from knotting my sheets to escape out of the bedroom window if I want to have a night out! How can I get them to back off?*

A Studying is often a balancing act. On one side there are friends to distract you and on the other parents and family who might drive you to distraction! Parents often feel helpless and so resort to 'pep talk', however unwelcome. It's the old-school approach that hours spent locked away means hard work, and that will lead to success. Parents just need to know that you have it all under control or how they can help. Get them to back off by being upfront, but kind. Tensions will impact adversely on your mood, and will have a knock-on effect on studying. First, you need to work out how you can involve them in a way that supports you and second to tell them. Start by thanking them for their concern then explain your routine and let them know what helps, and what doesn't.

Learning is not just about the facts and figures. A large part is how we handle stress and manage relationships.

Learning principle

 Talk to your parents and let them know how they can help to support your studying.[2]

Connections and overlaps

 Carry on reading in order, choose one of the following or roll a dice:

1. Stress (Chapter 3, pp. 15–21)
2. Wellbeing (Chapter 4, pp. 23–30)
3. Emotions (Chapter 8, pp. 59–66)
4. Context (Chapter 7, pp. 51–57)
5. Revision (Chapter 11, pp. 87–94)
6. Techniques (Chapter 9, pp. 67–75)

E: Letter to a concerned parent

Q *Our son is struggling with exam revision and we're at a loss as to how we can help him. In my day, we were just told to 'grin and bear it'. He's moody, locks himself away in his bedroom for hours but says that nothing's going in. I've notice that all the corners of his books seem to have been chewed off too. I don't think I was ever that bad. What can we do to help him?*

A When someone would rather eat their books rather than read them, it's a sign that things need to change! When revising for exams, it's easy to go 'stir crazy' and fall into a routine of boredom, tiredness, and sheer frustration. Mood swings are par for the course. Resist the temptation to try to police the situation or offer pep-talks. However well intentioned, it might have the opposite effect. The best you can do is be there and just listen. Rather than try to give solutions, ask what you can do to support them. Often, just being a 'sounding board' will be enough.

We all process information better when we are relaxed, so aim to be a calming influence. It might seem motivating to talk about getting good grades. But, it will just add to the stress and make it more difficult for him to study.

Overcoming the habit of solitary confinement might take a little negotiation. Let your son know that you're there to help in any way. Encourage him to join at least one family meal a day. Perhaps a good breakfast to kick start the day. Stocking up the fridge with healthy snacks is an effective way to lure him into the kitchen. Pick your moment and ask about the best times for breaks, drinking water, getting a bit of fresh air and enough sleep.

'Walking on eggshells' can be stressful. So, it's vital you look after yourself too by finding ways and the time to relax. This plan will have a knock-on effect on the whole house and will help more than any pep-talk.

Learning principle

Parents can help the most by listening, staying calm and avoiding pep-talks.[3]

Connections and overlaps

Carry on reading in order, choose one of the following or roll a dice:

1. Revision (Chapter 11, pp. 87–94)
2. Stress (Chapter 3, pp. 15–21)

3. Wellbeing (Chapter 4, pp. 23–30)
4. Context (Chapter 7, pp. 51–57)
5. Emotions (Chapter 8, pp. 59–66)
6. Motivation (Chapter 5, pp. 31–40)

Summary and what's next

Knowing when you need help, who to ask, and how to ask are not optional add-ons. Building a support network is a key part of the whole learning experience and an important lesson for life. Letting other people help you gives you first hand experience of how you you'll be able to pass it on when it's your turn to help others.

If you've read the book from cover to cover, you're almost at the end apart from a summary of the main principles and the 'Outro'.

Oh, and the exam.

Checklist

Keep a track of which letters you've read.

A Read it ☐
B Read it ☐
C Read it ☐
D Read it ☐
E Read it ☐

SUMMARY OF LEARNING PRINCIPLES

Your 12-point summary of 'learning how to learn'

The 12 main principles in this book form three groups plus one overarching theme.

A. The guiding principle (1).

B. Laying the foundations – *to get fit and ready to learn* (2, 3 and 4).

C. Managing obstacles – *to have a less bumpy ride* (5, 8 and 12).

D. Practical psychology – *for the nitty-gritty, 'nuts and bolts'* (6, 7, 9, 10 and 11).

Twelve principles of learning how to learn

1. Use the basic principles of learning how to learn to create an approach that's effective and *meaningful to you.*

2. Adopt positive mental attitudes to frame your experiences and to process information more efficiently (Chapter 2 – Attitudes).

3. Be pro-active and make a habit of actively relaxing to reduce stress (Chapter 3 – Stress).

4. Work with the body–mind connection – supporting your academic performance and moods as you take care of your general wellbeing (Chapter 4 – Wellbeing).

5. Use tools and techniques to boost and maintain your motivation (Chapter 5 – Motivation).

6. Work with psychology rather than against it – work smarter not harder (Chapter 6 – Cognition).

7. Create a positive learning environment and a predictable routine to aid memory and learning (Chapter 7 – Context).

8. Take control and manage your moods and emotional ups and downs rather than let them 'manage' you (Chapter 8 – Emotions).

9. Engage with the subject matter through active learning strategies instead of passive approaches (Chapter 9 – Techniques).

10. For assignments, do things 'by the book' and get the basics right rather than trying to do your own thing (Chapter 10 – Assignments).

11. Create a varied and interesting routine for exam revision based on key principles in psychology (Chapter 11 – Revision).

12. Be clear with other people about how they can support you and ask for help when you need it (Chapter 12 – Support).

A BIT OF
AN OUTRO ...

A note on who gets the final word

For most people, the tactics in this book will be enough. These principles have served me well, personally and professionally. I have used them, over the years, in learning skills tutorials and with academic coaching clients. They offer a blueprint for learning how to learn and have helped countless students along the way. They also offer great tenets to live by. But reading is only half the story. It's what you do with the different view that counts.

You might want to delve deeper to uncover advanced learning techniques for even more of an edge. I'm apt to think that it might be a case of the law of diminishing returns. You could put in a lot of effort for minimal gains. But don't let me put you off. Just make sure it doesn't take you away from actually studying. Will it help you to tap into the joy of learning, make the process more meaningful, support your active engagement, reduce stress, and empower you? Does it support the principles you've learned from this book? Does it offer a good return on the effort gets results, if so, go for it! It's your journey.

As Dr Samuel Johnson (1709–1784), writer and lexicographer said, 'a writer only begins a book. A reader finishes it'.

So, just as you've made your own way through the book, you get the last word too! Make of it what you will.

It's your happy ending.

> *We lift ourselves by our thought, we climb upon our vision of ourselves. If you want to enlarge your life, you must first enlarge your thought of it and of yourself.*
> Orison Swett Marden (1848–1924),
> author

You should now feel empowered to take the exam . . .

THE EXAM

Questions to guide
your reading and ones you
should be able to answer
after reading this book

- Relax. Breathe. This exam is not compulsory. The use of this book is permitted. You have as much time as you need.

- Use the questions to guide your reading or to help sum-up the main takeaway points from this book.

- **Tip:** Link stuff from more than one chapter for each question.

1. Summarize three changes you could add to your learning approach to make it more interesting and meaningful to you.

2. How do your attitudes impact on how you learn and retain information?

3. What advice would you give to a student to ease stress and why?

4. How does lifestyle impact on wellbeing, mood, and learning?

5. What principles in psychology are more likely to help motivate you to get started and keep going?

6. Discuss three ideas from psychology you can use to boost your cognitive performance.

7. Outline three ways in which you can use context to support learning.

8. What could you do to take control of your study routine to help manage your mood and emotions?

9. Discuss the gains in using active learning methods rather than passive approaches.

10. Describe three ways in which you might limit your success on coursework assignments. What steps will you take to deal with them?

11. Outline a 12-point plan of exam revision tactics that works with psychology rather than fights it.

12. What support from other people do you need for your studies? What three key things could you do to help yourself?

ABOUT THE AUTHOR

Dr Gary Wood is a Chartered Psychologist, solution-focused life coach and broadcaster. He is a Fellow of the Higher Education Academy and has taught psychology, research methods, and learning skills in several UK universities, at all levels. Gary is on The British Psychological Society's 'media-friendly psychologists' list and is widely quoted in the media offering expert analysis, quotes, and coaching tips and as a featured advice columnist (agony uncle) in magazines, on radio and television. As a consultant, he has worked on social policy research projects and reports, for government bodies, broadcasting regulators, health organizations, NHS Trusts, charities, and media companies. He has published in academic journals on a range of topics in and around psychology and is the author of several self-help books including *Don't Wait for Your Ship to Come In . . . Swim Out to Meet It*, which has been translated into several languages, and *Unlock Your Confidence*. He also wrote *The Psychology or Gender* for the first wave of Routledge's *The Psychology of Everything* series. Gary is in private practice as a personal and professional development coach, an academic coach, trainer, and research consultant, based in Birmingham and Edinburgh, UK. See www.drgarywood.co.uk.

GET IN
TOUCH ...

If you've enjoyed this book and want to discuss personalized one-to-one academic coaching with me, get in touch for a free consultation to discuss your needs. I also offer coaching for personal and professional development, face-to-face, by telephone or via the Internet. Email info@drgarywood.co.uk for more information.

For updates on blog posts, events and special offers please check out and subscribe to my website: www.drgarywood.co.uk or like my Facebook Page: www.facebook.com/drgarywoodpage. And, if you have any questions about anything in *Letters to a New Student*, don't be shy, just ask.

NOTES

If you want to dig a little deeper

Chapter 2 – Attitudes

1. For more on the psychology of first impressions see Vitelli, R. (2016). The science of making a better first impression . . . and why it matters so much. *Psychology Today*. Available at: www.psychology today.com/us/blog/media-spotlight/201605/the-science-making-better-first-impression Accessed 20/03/2018. For a complete course in confidence building see: Wood, G. (2013). *Unlock Your Confidence. Finding the Keys to Lasting Change with the Confidence-Karma Method.* London: Watkins.

    See Solomon Asch's (1946) research on halo effects in any introductory psychology textbook, such as Gross, R. (2015). *Psychology: The Science of Mind and Behaviour 7th Edition.* London: Hodder & Stoughton.

2. For more on the function of attitudes see Katz, D. (1960). The Functional Approach to the Study of Attitudes. *Public Opinion Quarterly, 24*, pp.163–204. See also Loftus and Palmer (1974) on how question wording affects recall of events, cited in Gross (2015).

3. Psychological hardiness has been well researched by Suzanne Kobasa and Salvatore Maddi since the 1970s. See: Kobasa, S. C. (1979). Stressful life events, personality, and health – inquiry into hardiness. *Journal of Personality and Social Psychology, 37* (1). pp.1–11.

4. Wood (2013).

Chapter 3 – Stress

1   In the treatment of phobias by systematic desensitization, the key principle is that anxiety and relaxation cannot co-exist. See the work of Joseph Wolpe – one of the most eminent psychologists of the twentieth century: Wolpe, J. (1991). *The Practice of Behavior Therapy*. Oxford: Pergamon Press. You'll find a review of his work in any introductory psychology textbook.

Relaxation is a key psychological skill for elite performance in sports psychology. See: Hardy, L., Jones, G., and Gould, D. (1996). *Understanding Psychological Preparation for Sport: Theory and Practice of Elite Performers*. Chichester: John Wiley & Sons.

The idea of building an association between the calmer mantra and the relaxation response is based on Classical Conditioning in psychology – the same idea as Pavlov's dogs, that is, a ringing bell becomes linked with feeding time. For a general discussion on strategies to combat stress see: Wood, G. (2008). *Don't Wait for Your Ship to Come In . . . Swim Out to Meet It! Tools and Techniques for Positive Lasting Change*. Chichester: Capstone.

2   For more on the Daily Hassles and Uplifts theory of stress see Kanner, A. D., Coyne, J. C, Schaefer, C., and Lazarus, R. S. (1981). Comparison of two modes of stress measurement: Daily hassles and uplifts versus major life events. *Journal of Behavioral Medicine*, *4* (1), pp.1–39.

3   For more on 'productive stress' see Yerkes R. M. and Dodson J. D. (1908). The relation of strength of stimulus to rapidity of habit-formation. *Journal of Comparative Neurology and Psychology*, *18*, pp. 459–482. See: https://onlinelibrary.wiley.com/doi/abs/10.1002/cne.920180503. Accessed 2/4/2018.

Chapter 4 – Wellbeing

1   For a review of the benefits of exercise on cognition, see: Martynoga, B. (2016). How physical exercise makes your brain work better. *The Guardian*, 18/06/2016. See: www.theguardian.com/education/2016/jun/18/how-physical-exercise-makes-your-brain-work-better. Accessed 29/3/2018.

For the effects of exercise on mood see: Weir, K. (2011). The exercise effect. *Monitor on Psychology*, 2 (11), p. 48. See: https://apa.org/monitor/2011/12/exercise.aspx. Accessed 4/4/2018. Also, Rhodes, J. (2013) Why do I think better after I exercise? *Scientific*

American. See: www.scientificamerican.com/article/why-do-you-think-better-after-a-walk-exercise/. Accessed 4/4/2018.

For more on wellbeing and confidence see: Wood, G. (2013). *Unlock Your Confidence*. London: Watkins.

2   For more on sleep loss and cognition see: Alhola, P., and Polo-Kantola, P. (2007). Sleep deprivation: Impact on cognitive performance. *Neuropsychiatric Disease and Treatment*, 3 (5), 553–567. See: www.ncbi.nlm.nih.gov/pmc/articles/PMC2656292/. Accessed 30/3/2018.

For more on sleep loss and mood see: Gordon, A. M. (2013). Up all night: The effects of sleep loss on mood. *Psychology Today*. See: www.psychologytoday.com/us/blog/between-you-and-me/201308/all-night-the-effects-sleep-loss-mood. Accessed 30/3/2018. See also, Zohar, D., Tzischinsky, O., Epstein, R., and Lavie, P. (2005). The effects of sleep loss on medical residents' emotional reactions to work events: A cognitive-energy model. *Sleep*, 28 (1), pp. 47–54.

For the links between sleep loss and eating patterns see: Quan, S. (2016). Could lack of sleep trigger a food 'addiction'? Harvard Health Blog. See: www.health.harvard.edu/blog/lack-sleep-trigger-food-addiction-201604069403. Accessed 30/3/2018.

For more on circadian rhythms see The National Sleep Foundation's website: https://sleepfoundation.org/sleep-topics/what-circadian-rhythm. Accessed 9/4/2018.

For other sleep-related articles check out the www.sleep.org.

3   Lieberman, H. R. (2013). Hydration and cognition: A critical review and recommendations for future research. *Journal of the American College of Nutrition*, 26. See: www.tandfonline.com/doi/abs/10.1080/07315724.2007.10719658. Accessed 30/3/2018.

4   Selhub, E. (2015) Nutritional psychiatry: Your brain on food. Harvard Health Blog. See: www.health.harvard.edu/blog/nutritional-psychiatry-your-brain-on-food-201511168626. Accessed 30/3/2018.

For a list of foods that impact on cognitive functions see: Gómez-Pinilla, F. (2008). Brain foods: The effects of nutrients on brain function. *Nature Reviews. Neuroscience*, 9 (7), pp. 568–578. http://doi.org/10.1038/nrn2421. Accessed 30/3/2018.

Chapter 5 – Motivation

1   For a summary of Maslow's Hierarch of Needs see: Wood, G. (2013). *Unlock Your Confidence. Finding the Keys to Lasting Change with the Confidence-Karma Method*. London: Watkins.

For more on breathing exercises see: Wood. G. (2008). *Don't Wait For Your Ship to Come In . . . Swim Out to Meet It! Tools and Techniques for Positive Lasting Change*. Chichester: Capstone.

2   For a review of the research on self-talk as a psychological skill in sport see: Hardy, L., Jones, G., and Gould, D. (1996). *Understanding Psychological Preparation for Sport: Theory and Practice of Elite Performers*. Chichester: John Wiley & Sons.

Both Wood (2008) and Wood (2013) have chapters on self-talk.

3   For more on this visualization techniques see Wood (2008) and Wood (2013). For a review of the research on visualization in sport see: See: Hardy and Gould (1996).

4   For more on SMART goals see Wood (2008).

Chapter 6 – Cognition

1   For a summary of learning theory see: Wood. G. (2008). *Don't Wait for Your Ship to Come In . . . Swim Out to Meet It! Tools and Techniques for Positive Lasting Change*. Chichester: Capstone.

Koren, M. (2013). B. F. Skinner: The man who taught pigeons to play ping-pong and rats to pull levers. See: www.smithsonian mag.com/science-nature/bf-skinner-the-man-who-taught-pigeons-to-play-ping-pong-and-rats-to-pull-levers-5363946/. Accessed 24/4/2018.

For a definition of learning see Lachman, S. J. (2010) Learning is a process: Toward an improved definition of learning. *The Journal of Psychology*, *131* (5), pp. 477–480, https://doi.org/10.1080/00223989 709603535. Accessed 6/5/2018.

2   Watson, L. (2015). Humans have shorter attention span than goldfish, thanks to smartphones. See: www.telegraph.co.uk/science/2016/03/12/humans-have-shorter-attention-span-than-goldfish-thanks-to-smart/. Accessed 06/05/2018.

Maybin, S. (2017). Busting the attention span myth, BBC News. See: www.bbc.co.uk/news/health-38896790 Accessed 06/05/2018.

For more on attention and 'The Cocktail Party Phenomenon' see: Wood, G. (2008).

3   For more on incubation see: Sio, U. N. and Ormerod, T. C. (2009). Does incubation enhance problem solving? A meta-analytic review. *Psychological Bulletin*, *135*, 1, pp. 94–120.

For more on the 'tip of the tongue' experience see Roberts-Grey, G. (2013). How to beat 'tip of the tongue' syndrome. See: www.next avenue.org/how-beat-tip-tongue-syndrome/. Accessed 28/3/2018.

For more on the 'broaden and build' theory and how relaxation aids creativity see: Fredrickson, B. L. (2004). The broaden-and-build theory of positive emotions. *Philosophical Transactions of the Royal Society: Biological Sciences, 359* (1449), pp. 1367–1378. See: www.ncbi.nlm.nih.gov/pmc/articles/PMC1693418/. Accessed 3/4/2018.

For the benefits of noise on creativity see: de Lange, C. (2013). Hacking our senses to boost learning power. BBC Future. See: www.bbc.com/future/story/20131022-hacking-senses-to-boost-learning. Accessed 28/4/2018.

For more on gender differences see Wood, G. W. (2018). *The Psychology of Gender*. Oxford: Routledge.

Chapter 7 – Context

1 For more on the effects of context on learning see: Bransford, J. D. and Johnson, M. K. (1972). Contextual prerequisites for understanding: Some investigations of comprehension and recall. *Journal of Verbal Learning and Verbal Behavior, 11*, 717–726.

2 For a general review of the effect of noise and music on performance see: Dalton, B .H. and Behm, D. G. (2007). Effects of noise and music on human and task performance: A systematic review. *Occupational Ergonomics, 7*, pp. 143–152.

For a review of research on the effects of classical music on learning see: Jakob Pietschnig, S., Martin Voracek, M. & Formann, A. K. (2010). Mozart effect-Shmozart effect: A meta-analysis. *Intelligence, 38* (3) pp. 314–323.

For the benefits of noise on creativity see: de Lange, C. (2013). Hacking our senses to boost learning power. BBC Future. See: www.bbc.com/future/story/20131022-hacking-senses-to-boost-learning. Accessed 28/4/2018.

3 Natasha Hinde, N. (2016). How to improve memory: Sniff rosemary and drink peppermint tea, study suggests. Huffington Post. www.huffingtonpost.co.uk/entry/how-to-improve-memory-smell-rosemary-and-drink-peppermint-tea_uk_5720847be4b06bf544e0eee8. Accessed 30/4/2018. And yes, there's the terrible joke; to remember, sniff Rosemary, but get her permission first.

Moss, M., Earl, V., Moss, L., and Heffernan, T. (2017) Any sense in classroom scents? Aroma of rosemary essential oil significantly improves cognition in young school children. *Advances in Chemical Engineering and Science, 07* (04). pp. 450–463.

Chapter 8 – Emotions

1   For this and other practical techniques see Wood. G. (2008). *Don't Wait for Your Ship to Come In . . . Swim Out to Meet It! Tools and Techniques for Positive Lasting Change*. Chichester: Capstone. See also: Wood, G. (2013). *Unlock Your Confidence. Finding the Keys to Lasting Change with the Confidence-Karma Method*. London: Watkins Publishing.

2   *Emotions and hopefulness:* For a complete review of the research and principles of explanatory styles see Seligman, M. (1998). *Learned Optimism: How to Change Your Mind and Your Life*. London: Free Press. For a brief review of 'learned optimism' see Wood. G. (2008) and Wood, G. (2013).

3   *Emotions and coping strategies:* See: Lazarus, R. S. and Folkman, S. (1984). *Stress, Appraisal, and Coping*. New York: Springer.

4   See more of the effects of adopting the attitude of control in Kobasa, S. C. (1979). Stressful life events, personality, and health – Inquiry into hardiness. *Journal of Personality and Social Psychology*, 37 (1), pp. 1–11. See also: Lazarus and Folkman (1984).

Chapter 9 – Techniques

1   Stewart, L. (2018). 10 ways to take better lecture notes. Save the Student, www.savethestudent.org/extra-guides/take-better-lecture-notes-8-easy-steps.html Accessed 3/6/2018

   For a discussion on the subject of 'default lecture capture' see Cupples, J. (2018). Default lecture capture: In defense of academic freedom, safety and well-being. Visit: www.juliecupples.wordpress.com/2018/08/27/default-lecture-capture-in-defense-of-academic-freedom-safety-and-well-being/ Accessed 4/9/2018.

   Crossley. K. (2015). How to make the best law lecture notes of all time. Survive Law. www.survivelaw.com/single-post/559-how-to-make-the-best-lecture-notes-of-all-time. Accessed 3/6/2018.

   For more on spider-diagrams see The Organic Mind website: www.the-organic-mind.com/spider-diagrams.html. Accessed 3/6/2018.

   For more on Mind Maps invented by Tony Buzan, see: www.tonybuzan.com/

2   The SQ3R system was devised by Francis Pleasant Robinson's in his 1970 book *Effective Study* (New York: Harper & Row). Summaries are widely available on-line. There are alternative versions such as the PQRST method.

Chapter 10 – Assignments

1 For a full account of the Loving Kindness Mediation see: www. buddhanet.net/metta_in.htm. Accessed 4/6/2018. See also Tierney, E. (1998). *101 Ways to Better Communication*. London: Kogan Page.

Chapter 11 – Revision

1 The 'fantasy lecture' technique brings together principles from a number of chapters, including the idea of 'good stress' from Chapter 3 and actively making connections (see Chapter 6 on Cognition and Chapter 9 on Techniques).

2 For more on dealing with boredom (see Chapter 3 on Stress, Chapter 5 on Motivation and Chapter 8 on Emotions).

3 For more information on time management and 'playing by the rules' (see Chapter 5 on Motivation, Chapter 9 on Techniques and Chapter 10 on Assignments).

Chapter 12 – Support

1 Byrom, N. (2016). *How to Cope with Student Life. MIND.* See: www.mind.org.uk/media/4041539/mind_how_to_cope_with_ student-life_web_2016.pdf. Accessed 26/5/2018.

   Frot, M. (2017). *How to Cope with Depression at University.* Top Universities. www.topuniversities.com/blog/how-cope-depression-university. Accessed 26/5/2018. Swift, S. (2016). *Depression at University: Feeling Alone and How to Cope when Studying Abroad.* Student.com. www.student.com/articles/depression-at-university-studying-abroad/. Accessed 26/5/2018.

2 After you've finished this book, give it to your parents to read.

3 Webb, A. (2016). Exam stress – Tips for parents. The Spark. www.thespark.org.uk/exam-stress-tips-parents-students/. Accessed 31/5/2018. See also Exam stress. Reachout.com. http://ie.reachout. com/parents/wellbeing/school-college/exam-stress/#. Accessed 31/ 5/2018.

INDEX